Faith, Guts, Action

A Step-By-Step Guide for Your Business Success

Faith, Guts, and Action

A Step-By-Step Guide for
Your Business Success

By Anna M. Jackson

Dedication

This book is dedicated to my mentor and friend, Mrs. Mary James Anderson.

You taught us how to start our business endeavor and you taught us the importance of having *faith on fire*. You believed in us from the day we met, more than we believed in ourselves. You allowed us to borrow your belief until we were strong enough to hold our own. It is because of your commitment, your love, and your desire to give back to the universe that our roots — your roots — have grown into trees. These trees continue to grow, bear fruit, and multiply. Thank you for never giving up on us. Your love, your prayers and your living example kept us growing.

We are forever grateful for your beam of light. We love you.

Table of Contents

Foreword

Each of us can reflect on our lives and remember those specific turning points in which something happened that forever changed us. In *Think and Grow Rich for Women*, I wrote about one of my own turning points, when, at the young age of twenty-five I made the decision to leave public accounting and follow my entrepreneurial dreams to start and build businesses. It wasn't an easy decision for me. As I sat on my bed reviewing my list of pros and cons, it was as if a higher power took over my hand and wrote the words "Why Not?" across the top of the page.

I asked myself, *why not? Why not give it a try? Why not see where this exciting opportunity takes me? Why not take the road less traveled?* These words have become the guiding principle of my own life: Why not?

I can certainly relate to this book, *Faith, Guts, and Action*. Anna Jackson focuses on putting your Faith and Guts into Action, knowing there are infinite possibilities to achieve that goal. I say to you, Why Not?

Disruption is not an easy way to describe a situation when someone finally comes into knowing that they must make a change in their life. In this book, Anna shares the path she and her husband have taken in a quest to gain financial freedom and to live their dreams through starting their own business by opening a Beauty School. Anna describes in detail their struggle from being unemployed and on welfare to building a multiple seven-figure business within three years, and then taking their dream and knowledge to Africa. She speaks of her "Why," that which compelled them to think differently, to take action, to move in a direction they had never gone before.

Their perspective shifted from an employee's point of view to a position of business ownership. That seemed an impossible feat for many others like them. Anna speaks of the huge mistakes they made, the embarrassing moments, the tough decisions and their willingness to stay focused, no matter what!

This book is about moving forward *fearlessly* with a sense of knowing that there will be times of economic downturn, failed attempts, disappointment, struggle, frustration, and darkness. There were even times that her dream seemed impossible. She describes her passion, drive, and motivation to succeed that allowed her to overcome the naysayers and negative environment she and her husband found themselves in.

Anna shares the valuable lessons she learned along her journey, that even with no way of seeing the light, she knew without a doubt that something would show up and present itself in a way that would allow her to succeed.

Unfortunately, many people go through life with dreams that never see the light of day for fear of losing something or fear of failure if they try. This does not have to be your reality. Anna knows because she has been there, done that. Not once, but twice.

We have answers around us every day. There are systems in place; there is technology ready to be utilized. We see proof on our way to work every day of successful entrepreneurs who have made the decision to move forward. There is an answer to every obstacle that holds us back. Your dreams are waiting to manifest, there are people seeking you, and there are always new lessons to be learned.

Anna and her husband have lived an adventure that not only allowed them the success they sought, but also allowed them to be significant in the lives of others.

This isn't a book about relaxing another minute thinking about what you should do, but rather taking action today toward realizing your dreams, doing what is in your heart. Start now with *Faith, Guts, and Action.*

Why not you? Why not now?

To your success!

Sharon Lechter CPA CGMA

Author of *Think and Grow Rich for Women,* Co-author of *Outwitting the Devil, Three Feet From Gold* and *Rich Dad Poor Dad*

Preface

Our story is a story of hard work and an incredible amount of learning. It is a story of heartbreaking setbacks and the overcoming of adversity. It is a story of wonderful people who strove with us to build — and rebuild — a business. It is also a story of faith, but a special kind of faith that I call *faith on fire*.

What is *faith on fire*?

It is hard to define if you haven't felt it yourself, but here are some characteristics that may help you understand:

- It is having sight beyond your eyes and hearing beyond your ears.

- It is knowing that there is a power greater than you.

- It is a knowledge that is unrelated to mental capacity or clarity.

- It is not dependent on physical makeup.

- It is a concept that is beyond our thinking minds; it cannot be understood this way.

- Faith makes the impossible possible. It is not explainable using logic or reason.

Faith on its own has great power. You may describe *faith on fire* as the combining of faith with burning desire. There is no more powerful force.

Do you know how small a mustard seed is? Probably just a little bigger than the bullet points in the section above. It is said that just having the faith of a mustard seed will move mountains. Imagine the strength of faith combined with burning desire!

If you are reading this book, it may be because you are contemplating a new phase in your life. Do you feel insecure and uncertain? Do you feel afraid to take a chance on yourself?

It will take practice to undo all of the negative programming that has left you tied in knots. It will take determination and hard work to battle procrastination, insecurity, and laziness. But if you have *faith on fire*, you will succeed.

I have never claimed to be religious, although I do feel that I am a spiritual person. One thing that I know for sure is that there is a God who moves throughout our lives. God has opened doors for me that I didn't ask for; I didn't even imagine them. These were not my plans; they came through God's hands.

I understand now that this kind of divine intervention takes place once you make a decision. It takes you in the direction you need to go in to receive the results you seek. Having faith and putting forth the effort will drive you to your destiny.

Do you feel like you must toil and labor to receive the blessings that you deserve?

This is not so; these blessings do not come from the outside. Greatness already lies within you. You just have to access it.

You can decide to struggle or to have a life full of abundance. It is your choice. The circumstances in which we find ourselves are a direct result of our thoughts and decisions. You have all the tools within you to accomplish your heart's desire, to bring to fruition the dreams that have lain dormant due to fear.

God loves you no matter what you have done, no matter what mistakes you have made in the past—or the ones you will make in the future. If you take a step in faith, I can tell you from my own experience that help will arise to assist you in your journey. Just make the move and do not procrastinate. Don't worry; whatever move you make is the right move. Just *move!* You have a covenant with God! He is your strength! You *cannot* fail.

God will see you through even the most difficult times you are faced with.

I didn't know what would happen when I began my journey. I didn't know that I would end up in places that God created just for me. I did not expect it nor see it coming. I only stayed open to possibility.

I cannot begin to tell you the miracles that have happened to Preston and me over the years; words could never explain. I know that there is a God who gives us vision and ability. I know that, when an idea comes into your mind, it is put there for you, by a higher power, for you to manifest.

These are *your* dreams. Bring them forth!

Acknowledgments

To my mother, Lorraine Cheney. You have always believed in me. Thank you for teaching me to have faith and to believe. Thank you for praying for me relentlessly; your prayers were answered over and over again.

To my daughter, Lakia; my son-in-law, Rick; my son, Preston; and my daughter-in-law, Kimmie: you all consistently rise above and beyond the call of duty with an incredible work ethic. Your collective skills in business, technology, marketing, strategy, and life balance were essential for us to build a multi-million dollar business. You have encouraged, inspired, and supported me in everything I do, and you always remind me of *the power within* when I meet challenges. I am grateful to have you as partners and friends. You have worked relentlessly to build our business to a standard we can all be proud of. And you have kept our business ship afloat while I was on this mission of book writing. With all you do, you still find a way to include me too. Watching you inspires me to look for the joy in every moment.

To Kellee Patterson, my best friend forever—my BFF—who helped to read and reread chapters very carefully, adding editing touches that I completely missed: you expertly helped to craft this book, adding perspective where it was most needed. You know my work inside and out; not only did you understand and respect my message, you were passionate about getting it done from day one. Your enthusiasm encouraged and inspired me throughout the process.

I am eternally grateful to James and Kimberly Smith, with whom I discussed early ideas for the book and who graciously pushed and inspired me to create a supplementary presentation and workshop.

To my siblings and their spouses, Jerry, Heidi, Carmella, Delphine, Sylvester, Michael, and Patricia; and to all of my nieces, nephews, wives, and family: thanks for your love, encouragement, and support. Our love for each other has never wavered. Our close relationship is a testament to our strength and unconditional love. You are all precious and priceless to me.

To my grandchildren, Tanae, Love, Kai, RJ, Larae, and Lashae: thank you for interrupting my days with laughter and play. Thank you for reminding me that the journey is just as important as reaching the goal.

As Stevie Wonder wrote:

> *You are the sunshine of my life, that's why I'll always be around.*
> *You are the apple of my eye, forever you'll stay in my heart!*

And, finally, the most important recognition must be reserved for my husband, Preston Jackson. Preston, you worked tirelessly to support our dream of building a business. You are a pillar of strength. Thank you for enduring all of the frustrations, the letdowns, the problems, sleepless nights, and the sacrifices that had to be made to achieve our dream. Even when it didn't look promising, you kept going. Our lives are better because we changed our minds about our world and we created the world we wanted to live in. You are my greatest teacher.

I am eternally grateful for your love, support, and patience. Thank you for believing in me and in our dream.

Introduction

My husband, Preston, and I have often been asked questions like:

- What inspired you to become entrepreneurs?

- What are the most valuable lessons you learned on your way to becoming successful?

I have struggled with responding to these questions because no single answer could encompass all that I wanted to say. There was so much that I wished I had known before starting our business! During our thirty years as entrepreneurs, we had learned a multitude of lessons.

As I thought about these lessons, the memories flowed vividly, and I began to write my thoughts. *Faith, Guts, and Action* was born of these thoughts, from my personal experiences, and from my observations, interviews, and lectures. Of course, the content also reflects the wisdom of my mentors over the years.

This is not a one-size-fits-all book of ideas but rather a compilation of lessons and best practices to ponder. My goal has been to extract the information that Preston and I found most beneficial and to identify the specific lessons that most allowed us to expand our thinking, to foster the growth of our business, and ultimately, to bring awareness and opportunities to others.

I have coached business owners for many years and what I have found is that successful people do what works and they keep on doing it. They maintain standards in their businesses that are not compromised by unsuccessful behavior. They do not re-invent the wheel; they tweak the wheel.

Accordingly, many of the ideas in this book are not new; they were invented long ago and have been time-tested. For our business, we chose the ideas we could best grow from, to tweak for our particular needs. Each business is different and will require different strategies. We learned to study the experts and select appropriate tactics for our purposes. This wisdom has saved me time and trouble and helped me to overcome many of the hurdles that new businesses go through.

Do you wish for the opportunity to open your own business?

If so, this book is written for you.

It may be difficult to take that first step to get yourself started in the business world. It isn't uncommon to feel scared and intimidated, but if it is your dream, you must pursue it. I have met too many wishful entrepreneurs who never even began because they were afraid. I have met others who researched and planned their business for years, but kept procrastinating and eventually gave up completely.

I wrote *Faith, Guts, and Action* to help other people rise above their fears, to get off of the fence and move into the direction of their passion.

It is my hope that in this book you can find something that resonates within you, that will inspire you to let go of what is holding you back so that you can build the business of your dreams on the back of your passion.

Throughout this book you will find stories from the road we took and lessons we learned along the way. Your journey will be different, of course, but some of the tips you read you will be able to apply immediately. Other ideas may be helpful to you later as your business grows.

In addition, in the Appendix, you will find a series of worksheets that will help you begin your journey and guide you toward your goals.

Are you still procrastinating? Let's begin the journey together!

Chapter One

The Entrepreneurial Mindset

WHAT IS YOUR MINDSET?

A Sideways Mind in a Traditional World

Consider the two scenarios below. One describes a weekday in the life of a traditional employee and the other describes the same day in the life of somebody who is self-employed.

Scenario one:

Your alarm goes off at 5:30 a.m. You stumble to the coffee pot and then to the shower. You're out the door by 7:00. Maybe you had to drop your children off at day-care first. You commute to work, stalled in a traffic jam that makes you late for your first meeting, where you snooze or play *Words with Friends* during the boring presentation.

You get home by 6:00 p.m. and start dinner, do laundry, and walk the dog. You watch the news and fall asleep by 10:00. The next morning, your alarm goes off at 5:30. This cycle goes on and on, five days a week, nearly every week of the year.

Scenario two:

Your alarm goes off. It's 7:30 a.m. You stumble to the coffee pot. After it brews you sit outside on your patio in the warm sun, thinking about your day. It is spring, and you take the time to smell the lilacs you had time to prune this year. You take your dogs for a walk.

You get back and start your workday, doing something you love instead of fighting traffic to go to a place you hate. You take a break for lunch to meet with some friends. You feel refreshed after you return home, so you work at your dining-room table for the rest of the afternoon, able to complete your project. You'll get paid today upon completion of your project instead of waiting two weeks. You feel good about life. You feel validated and fulfilled.

Which scenario do you like better?

If you choose scenario two, then read further to get closer to your dream!

Of course, an entrepreneur has a great deal of responsibility, and often has to work hard to get a business going and, at times, to keep a business going—as you will read in the upcoming chapters. The scenario described above is what a self-employed person might experience after their business is well-established.

You've thought about becoming an entrepreneur many times, haven't you? You find yourself sitting in your cubicle at work wondering what life would be like if you were working at home. Maybe you picture yourself painting a masterpiece or writing a memoir.

"But wait," you ask, "what about money? Who's going to pay the bills?"

You may be able to get rid of your boring job but you can't get rid of your bills like a magician vanishes a coin. The bill collectors won't understand your apologies; they simply won't care.

There are many other considerations as well, and it is easy to find a reason to stay where you are. You feel safe in your job.

But are you happy?

Are you using your gifts?

Do you go to work with joy in your heart?

Please note that I am not discouraging traditional work for everyone. Many people work well in a structured environment. And I commend those who do. Without the skilled efforts of those who can work well in regulated arenas, it would be extremely difficult for any entrepreneur to survive.

This book is for people who are wired like I am. I cannot be contained. Not everyone is cut out to work 9 to 5. For me, my brain sort of goes sideways after a while.

Does this describe you?

In our society, those who cannot or do not want to conform to routine, rules, and regulations are misfits; we think outside the box and so, do not fit in the traditional world of conformity and structure. We must create our own mechanism for achievement.

Don't knock us. With proper guidance, passion, and inspiration, we are likely to be very successful at working for ourselves or with our fellow dreamers.

Epiphanies

I started out working traditional jobs. It was years before I figured out that I was not designed for this kind of structure. There were moments that stand out in my memory now as epiphanies: they were clues that told me that I needed a change:

- I was talked down to by my supervisor and told that I could not take a day off when my child was ill.

- I spoke with my supervisor once about a promotion. Because it meant a move to another department, she wouldn't help me; I was too dependable and she didn't want to lose me.

- I missed parent-teacher conferences because I had to work overtime. I also missed my daughter's Open House Day, which was a very important event to her. I told Lakia I would speak to her teacher on my next day off. She stood there crying. I knew I had let her down, and I promised myself I would never do that again.

- I will never forget the time I was literally running to work because the bus was moving slower than I could run. I had just made it in the door, and was gasping for breath trying to hit the time clock when I saw a look of disapproval on my supervisor's face.

I knew that something needed to change. Working this kind of job would never be my ticket to freedom. I knew I must do something different.

I started dreaming about a new kind of life; I started thinking about what it would be like for my family and me if I started my own business and worked for myself.

Why Work For Yourself?

Here are some reasons other people have given for deciding that they didn't want to work for someone else. Do any of them ring true for you?

- *I loved my last job because I was doing something that I knew was perfect for me, but what I didn't like was the gossiping going on all day amongst the employees. I like to work alone.*

- *I worked for over ten years with the same employer and was never given a raise.*

- *My supervisor found a way to fire me when she saw the owner was giving me more attention. But, I later realized that they did me a favor. I wish they had done it sooner because I started my own business. And I would never have it any other way.*

- *All I know is I can't stand sitting at a desk all day just because someone is paying me to do so.*

- *I wish my boss would just give me a task with a goal and a deadline to complete and let me finish the assignment on my own time. I could be so much more creative and productive. But they want to tie me to a desk for the day with a coffee break and a lunch hour. This is not a lifestyle; it's a life sentence. I don't want to be caged.*

- *I'm tired of doing the same thing over and over again.*

- *I'm not paid what I am worth.*

- *I feel stuck in my job. I want to be self-employed but I don't know where to start. I need my own ideas I can develop into a business. I want more flexibility.*

- *I don't have any benefits or job security. Opportunities to build a legacy for my family are few.*

- *I'm not creating anything for myself. I don't want to spend the next twenty to thirty years hitting multimillion-dollar corporate targets to help them reach their goals, without creating anything for myself.*

- *Every time I leave for a vacation, I can't wait for the next one. I have no time to enjoy my home or my family. My job brings no challenge, excitement or purpose to my life.*

- *When my child — who is a straight A student — asked me why I can't ever take time off to come to see him perform in a school play, I knew then that I was compromising my responsibility as a parent.*

- *I am tired of going on job interviews and hoping they will pick me. Should I stand a certain way? Should I look them in the eye? Will I answer the question the way they want to hear it? Will they call me back? I am tired of looking at the guy who feels he can push the button to my future. I want to push my own button.*

- *Over twenty-five years of working a job, my workdays were routine and my earnings were consistent but I never had enough money to live a quality lifestyle. Before I knew it, my kids were grown. I lost time that I cannot get back. I couldn't spend time with loved ones who are now no longer here. I had spent my time in places where I didn't want to be.*

- *I wish I had followed my passion years ago and had become self-employed. I never liked the work I did, but I thought it would be insane to walk away from a good job that gave me a regular salary. I was wrong.*

- *At work, I am always thinking about how I can do something better or how I can develop some product or technique. I am always thinking about what I would do if I owned the business.*

- *I am not a timely person, usually late — still working on that. I don't make commitments because I like to live on my own terms.*

- *I don't want to set a date to return from a vacation or something I'm enjoying in the moment. I take risks and I enjoy the ride. I know I can work under pressure and challenge myself to excellence! I am spur-of-the-moment and have always wanted to work for myself, but didn't know where to start.*

- *I was not guided or trained to do my job. I was just thrown in on day one with no direction, and the boss left me alone to figure it out. I thought it was fine to do it the way I thought it should be done, but then my boss yelled at me and let me go. I really thought I was doing what he asked. Without training, I misunderstood his vision. I was disappointed and felt unappreciated. I ended up training my replacement.*

DO YOU REALLY WANT TO OWN YOUR OWN BUSINESS?

What are your reasons for wanting to open a business?

Owning your own business can be rewarding for many different reasons; every person's motivation will be a little different.

Remember, your reasons to become an entrepreneur do not have to be validated by anyone. If you don't get approval from those around you, don't let that keep you from your dream. Don't worry about the naysayers. Opening a business is certainly not for everyone.

If you talk to five different people and tell them you are thinking about starting your own business, you may receive five completely different reasons why they think it's a bad idea — or a good idea. Different people have different needs and different opinions.

Below you will find a list of the five most commonly cited benefits of owning your own business. Yours may be different, but they are no less valid.

Five Benefits of Owning Your Own Business

1. You Want to Reap Your Own Rewards

You know that if you don't work, you don't get paid. But you also realize that when you own your own business and work hard, you will reap the rewards yourself. You can make as much money as you decide you are willing to work for. You are a self-motivated person and this quality goes a long way in the entrepreneurial world. When you stay motivated and passionate about what you are doing, you can work hard during the hours you dedicate to your business, and you can also play hard as a reward to yourself.

2. Working for Yourself Is Challenging

When you work in the corporate world, you may well work long hours, even working through your lunch hour or staying late. Yet, you are rarely challenged. It's mundane and routine. With your own business, because you will be doing what you love, you are passionate and you feel challenged. You thrive on the rush of success.

3. You Can Have Pride in Your Accomplishments

In your business, your accomplishments result from your own initiative and hard work. You deserve to be proud. Your pride in your successes will affect every aspect of your life. Your family will see it; you will have a new attitude about life in general. Your friends will see it and want to be a part of it. Pride is squashed in the corporate world; we are either seen as arrogant or backstabbing. With your own business, you have every right to be proud of your own hard work.

4. Health Issues

Working a job that you dislike and following a schedule that is in conflict with your family life is stressful. If you start your own business and create a schedule that works for you, you will have more time to exercise and walk and be out in the fresh air. You won't feel the stress of the corporate world in your neck and shoulders. If you do what you love, you will be challenged and rewarded. All of these elements will reduce stress in your life, which can have great health rewards for you. You will feel great!

5. Balancing Working Life and Family Life

When you work 9 to 5, there are many things in life that can be difficult to schedule, like medical appointments and children's school activities. Owning your own business can be time-flexible. Have a dental appointment at 11:00 a.m.? No problem; you can go to your dentist appointment and work in the afternoon. You will no longer have to miss school and family events because you can set your own schedule.

ADOPTING THE ENTREPRENEURIAL MINDSET

For many years I have worked with business owners who were starting their business from scratch. Many of them were starting over, intending to move from one business into another; some of them were starting their very first business. Some were new graduates, some retirees, and some were seasoned business owners.

What did they all have in common?

They all wanted a better life.

Some of them were able to strap on their boots, get started, and build a successful business on a part-time basis while continuing to work another job. Others would talk a lot and make one excuse after another. They never got started.

They were missing a key element:

Beginning a new venture requires a change of mindset.

When you change your mind, you will change your focus; this is the only way to change your world.

The entrepreneurial mindset is positive. It is practical. It must focus on how you are going to proceed. If you are focused on limitations and excuses, you will not be able to take the first step. No amount of mentoring or coaching can help.

Think about your own mindset.

Are you ready to begin?

Chapter Two

Faith on Fire

COULD I DO IT ALL?

For years I wondered what it would be like if I actually stepped out in pursuit of my dream of being an entrepreneur. I wondered if I had the talent to make it work.

Could it happen for me?

Are you having similar thoughts?

Do you watch others from afar and wonder how they do it?

You see they own fine cars or a beautiful home on a hill; you see them wearing clothing that makes them look regal. You hear about those who travel around the world.

You wonder: *How can I have a life like that?*

I wondered too. Nobody in my family had ever lived that kind of lifestyle. Everyone I knew worked for someone else and lived paycheck to paycheck. There was usually just enough income to get by.

Instead of talking about their amazing lives, the people around me were always talking about what they *couldn't* afford to do or have. To go on a trip or to buy a car, we all had to save up for quite a while. Our lifestyles were designed around weekly budgets that were set based on our weekly paychecks.

We dreamed about buying the car of our dreams, not just the one we settled for. We dreamed about coming up with a new idea that could transform the world.

But then, every time I came up with an idea, I thought: *If this was really a good idea, wouldn't someone else have come up with it by now?*

Have you ever had this thought?

Fears and Doubts

I had many fears. Over the years I had heard about all the pressures and struggles that come with business ownership and doubted my ability to handle them.

I wondered:

- *What if I couldn't find enough clients?*
- *What if I couldn't keep up with the bills?*
- *Could I actually be successful running a company?*
- *Can I afford to hire the help I would need?*
- *Can I juggle a job, a business, and my home life?*
- *Can I do it all?*

Each time I had a business idea, I would stay bogged down by my doubts and questions and wouldn't even begin to pursue it. Then, one day, I would see an advertisement—someone else had used the very idea I had come up to create their own business!

Someone else was becoming wealthy because they took a chance. Meanwhile, I continued to feel dissatisfied and uncertain.

This state of mind creates resentment.

You may be resentful that someone else was using an idea that you should have used yourself. In addition, you may resent your current employer for requiring you to do tasks you don't want to do, for keeping you to a schedule, for not giving you days off so you can spend time with your family. You may resent your family responsibilities as well.

In reality, these resentments all come from another source: you resent yourself. You resent yourself for not taking the steps to improve your life.

There are an infinite supply of reasons not to try something new. *Too tired,* we say. *No time* — we've got too many things to do. *Too scared* — we are afraid of losing the little that we have. It is an endless cycle of fear.

Fear holds us back from our true freedom, the freedom that is waiting for each and every one of us who dares to take that step of entrepreneurship for ourselves. Once you do it, you will never be the same. I know because I did it!

I will tell you about each stage of our journey and the challenges we encountered. In each case, I will answer the questions I imagine you would ask:

What were we thinking?

What did we do? What strategies did we use?

What lessons did we learn along the way?

MAKING THE TOUGH DECISIONS

Our Quest for Freedom

My husband, Preston, worked at a job he absolutely hated. He would look at his watch and count down the minutes he had left to sit with me before he had to be on the assembly line at the factory. His face and skin absorbed, through his pores, the dirty oils from mechanical engines and metal machinery daily. He inhaled the fumes during the extreme heat of the sweltering hot summers. Breathing became difficult. People referred to it as *a good job.* And in those days, people worked hard to keep those jobs.

We had one child and one on the way while I was attending beauty school part-time. I worked as a tray girl in the kitchen of a hospital delivering food and snacks to the patients.

We lived in the attic at my brother-in-law's house, working to pay rent, have groceries, a car, and to occasionally go to a movie or out to dinner.

Did we have hopes and dreams?

Yes, we did! Doesn't everybody?

But how could we succeed, with children to care for, no formal education and no special skills?

We had followed the advice of our parents and other people around us. Their dream was to earn enough money to pay their bills and to hope that they could hold on to their jobs long enough to retire. That was our idea in the beginning. But fate had other plans for us.

I was nine months pregnant when I was fired from my job. Shortly afterward, Preston was also let go from his job. Our savings began to steadily diminish, and we were devastated, not knowing what to do or where to turn.

Unqualified, Underwater, and Scared

For the next few years we were going from one low-paying job to the next, constantly looking in the newspaper for a better one. Without education or influence, and only minimal skills, we discovered that there were very few positions that we were qualified for. We certainly didn't qualify for the jobs that would challenge us to use our creativity or talent.

Many of the jobs paid very little and involved being treated with rudeness and disrespect. There was little opportunity for advancement and no guarantee that the job would be permanent. Everything was routine; a controlled environment. You just showed up and worked. There was a long line of other people looking for these jobs as well.

Over time, it became apparent that our combined income wasn't enough to support us. Our last resort was to apply for welfare. Now, although we appreciated the fact that there was a system in place for times like these, we were very unhappy to be in this position. I left my case worker's office feeling miserable, worried, and frustrated. I felt that I didn't matter; that I was of no value. I was at the lowest point in my life.

We Didn't See It Coming

We were scared. For the first time in our lives, Preston and I were scared to death. We had no idea what direction our lives were going to take. We began to reflect deeply about how we arrived in these circumstances. Without steady employment, I had time to think about how we got there.

At only twenty-five years of age, my life had spiraled out of control.

We had known others who had gone through this kind of hardship, but never thought it would happen to us. We chose to ignore the signs. We never thought about investments or other options as a backup plan. We had been taught to just get what was considered a good job and keep it—and that had been our plan—but after years of being unhappy at our jobs, we had lost them both.

Now that there was time to reconsider all of my decisions that had led to this crisis, I came to the conclusion that I wanted to change our path. I wanted a better life.

I wanted to use the creative mind that God had given me to start my own business. At this point I knew that there was a business inside of me, but I didn't know what it would be. I had many fears. I wondered if we had enough brainpower, talent, and courage to get through the process.

The biggest, all-encompassing fear, however, was the possibility of remaining in the life we had—with no money, no stability, and no security. And for this reason alone, I knew that we had to build something of our own.

Considering the Price of Freedom

But I was no fool. I knew that with two children to support, our freedom would come with a hefty price tag. It would take sacrifice, money, commitment, discipline, pressure, and responsibility. It would also take time—and that was something that was already in short supply.

Having freedom would cost me time away from the lives of my young children and that was a big price to pay. But we needed to work to support our family, and we needed to strive to achieve a better living situation for all of us. It didn't matter what we had to do, because this time, it was about work with a purpose.

Everything felt different now. I felt deep down inside we were going to be fine. I kept that thought in my head and in my heart. I had the faith that we could do it, in spite of what it looked like at that moment. Something inside of me was on fire and burning to come out.

I've realized that a lot of people fail because of fear. They fear not doing a good job so they don't even try. To be great at something you have to do it over and over again until you get it right. Some things are not for everybody, this is true, but how will you know...if you don't even try?

~ Noelle Cooper

LIGHTING THE FIRE: A NEW MINDSET

Preston was eventually called back to the line job, and he appreciated the opportunity to have reliable work again. This time, though, we saw new possibilities. We were eager to get on with our lives.

I finished beauty school, became licensed, and worked in a salon building my skills. I was a very good cosmetologist and I loved what I did. We bought a new car and life went back to normal.

We sort of forgot about the idea of starting our own business, until the day came that we went to visit some friends. When we arrived at their home, they asked us to come to the backyard. They were cooking outside because their utilities were shut off in the house.

The wife came running to me, screaming excitedly, "Anna, I started a business! We have our own business now!"

They had opened a candy store. Although this may seem small to some, it was a great achievement to me. Personally, I had never known anyone who had opened a business. I couldn't sleep that night for thinking about it.

It had never occurred to me that she would be able to start a business. I had misjudged her based on her circumstances:

- No job
- Living on welfare
- Utilities shut off

Yet she had the confidence and the courage to do something I had been too afraid to try.

She had started a business. It didn't just lit a fire inside of me. It lit a *cannon* inside of me!

That was *my* dream! I'd always wanted to start a business but I once we became comfortable, I had just let the thought of it wither away.

The next morning, I woke up excited, my mind bursting with ideas. I was inspired by our friends.

I told Preston we were going to start our own business. I had decided I wanted to open a beauty salon.

Preston was simply happy that I was so happy. He looked at me and said, "Let's do it."

We knew there was a long road ahead of us. Fortunately for us, we were blessed to meet a lady by the name of Mrs. Mary James.

Chapter Three

Borrowing Belief

I DIDN'T KNOW ANYTHING ABOUT BUSINESS

When Preston and I made the decision to become entrepreneurs, we didn't have any formal education in business. We knew that we wanted to work for ourselves and we had to start putting it together somehow. We felt that we'd procrastinated long enough and didn't want to wait any longer to get started.

We needed a building to open a beauty salon so I put the word out, and I was given a referral from a friend for a woman who was looking to lease her building.

When I arrived at the building, I was greeted by an older woman. She had a friendly and perky personality. She asked me about my family, my goals, and my aspirations. This felt a little unusual but I found myself enjoying talking to her.

Then she stared right in my face for a moment, she backed up and smiled. She pointed her finger at me and said, "Baby, you need to open a beauty school."

Her name was Mrs. Mary James.

I told Mrs. James I didn't know anything about opening a business. I didn't have a college education or a degree. In fact, I barely graduated from high school.

BORROWING BELIEF FROM A MENTOR

She stopped me as I was ranting about how crazy it sounded for me to do something of this magnitude.

She shook her head forcefully, and then said, in a stern and serious tone, "Listen, I have been *there* and done *that* in this industry. I've owned one of the top beauty schools in the state. I have traveled and worked all over the world. I have done things you could not imagine. God owes me nothing! At this point in my life, the only way I can really see success again is through the eyes of others. I am willing to teach you if you are willing to learn."

I didn't know what to say. Nobody had ever offered me anything so generous.

I was so excited by her offer, but more important, by her belief in me. Although I was extremely grateful, I told her that I would have to talk with my husband first because he was expecting me to be finding a location for a salon. I was so ecstatic at the thought of something so grand that I couldn't wait to get home to talk to Preston about it.

I thought he would also be enthused about the idea but he wasn't as excited as I was.

Preston said, "Anna! First you wanted to open a salon, now you want to open a school? Come on! We don't know anything about opening a school. We don't have money for that! All we have is that income tax money and it's burning a hole in your pocket. Do you realize what you need to open a school? Teachers, Anna! We can't afford to pay a teacher's salary, pay for equipment and supplies! And you have to furnish a school. We don't know nothing about opening a business like that."

It did seem a far stretch of the imagination for someone like us.

I said, "Preston, I know we don't have the background but this lady said she will teach us. She said she owned a school before and she knows everything we will need to know. I know we don't have money but for some reason, I believe she can show us something that we don't know. Please, just come with me on Monday to meet her."

Although he was reluctant, to please me, he agreed to meet with her.

On the day that I took Preston to meet her, she came across as genuine to him as she did to me. The conversation she had with us about living a life of purpose made sense to both of us. If we made a success of our new business, Preston could visualize the exhausting drudgery of working at the factory coming to an end.

Mrs. James believed in us and although we really didn't know her, it felt like we could trust her. It seemed as though she believed in our ability more than our education, background, and finances. She believed in us more than we believed in ourselves.

So we *borrowed* her belief that it could be done.

Mrs. James inspired us to open our imagination to what life could be like if we could live our life on purpose by doing what we loved to do on our own terms by owning our own business. She became my mentor.

You know they say when the student is ready, the teacher will appear. I had no idea that I needed a mentor. I didn't foresee the benefits that would come of it. Little did I know then that this woman would completely change our lives.

VISUALIZING SUCCESS: A NEW CHAPTER BEGINS

When we finished talking, Mrs. James asked us to come outside with her. Together, we walked across the street and looked over at the building.

Mrs. James said, "I want you to visualize this school full of students coming and going in and out of that door."

I looked up at her and then I closed my eyes and proceeded to see her vision. We stood there for a moment. Suddenly, I could see it!

I opened my eyes and smiled at Mrs. James.

She said, "Baby, I want you to keep that vision in your head every day. See this school full of students."

I listened to her. I saw it. It was real. I believed it.

The next day, Mrs. James called and said, "Anna, I want you to dress in a dark business suit tomorrow. I am going to take you to Lansing because I want you to meet some people."

I didn't own a business suit, let alone a dark one. I didn't have the money to go out and buy one either, so I went to the Salvation Army and found a black suit and a white blouse and something that looked like a brief case.

I didn't know what to expect and I didn't feel prepared to have a business meeting. How would I have a conversation with people about something I didn't fully understand myself?

But that morning when I put on that suit and looked at myself in the mirror, briefcase in hand, I felt like I had stepped into the role of businesswoman. I was able to walk into the room with more pride and confidence than I expected to have.

And when Mrs. James introduced me to these influential leaders and industry professionals, she treated me with great respect, as though I was already a business professional.

And you know what? I felt like it!

At first, I was a little nervous being around these professional women in Lansing because I've never been in this position. I had never been in the company of powerful and successful leaders who thought I was one of them. It was an epic moment for me. I received instant credibility and favor by the women because they had so much respect for Mrs. James.

I began to loosen up and started chiming in on the conversations. I began to feel comfortable talking with them about my plans and my goals for the school. They made me laugh as we shared personal stories of life. Before I knew it, I was sure I was starting a new chapter in my life.

They gave me trade secrets, offered resources, and made suggestions. They referred clients to me. They took my number and connected me with other people who could provide advice and assistance. They even gave me their personal contact information so that I could call upon them whenever I needed to. Some of those relationships and connections are still with me today.

That was the first time I felt like I knew deep in my heart and soul that success was near. I was confident that we made the right decision to open the school and I couldn't wait to get home to tell my husband about my day.

When I demonstrated to him the professional way I had walked in with my briefcase, we both laughed.

Now it was time to begin.

Lessons Learned: Be Brave and Don't Waste Time

- Tomorrow is not promised to anyone. Do you have an idea that has been scrambling around in your head for a while now? Are you afraid to tell someone about it because you fear that if it leaks out, the idea is so awesome that someone will steal it, or you think its bad luck to bring it out before you are ready? Stop it! Make a decision to do this now and get all of the anxiety behind you.

- Every day that goes by without taking that small step toward your dream is wasting valuable, creative time. Do you want to have the time and financial freedom to live on your own terms? Be willing to do what it takes to achieve your goals, and start now rather than later.

- There will never be a perfect time to start your business. There will always be obstacles that will take you on a rollercoaster spin, but you will learn how to access the potential and resources waiting in that amazing brain you were born with.

Chapter Four

The Money Jugglers

GETTING STARTED

When we began to put our business together, we didn't have money to purchase new equipment or furnishings. The only money we had to start our business was two thousand dollars from our tax returns and we put that down on the building rental. After that was gone, everything else came from faith, commitment, belief, and a driving desire to get it done.

We were required by regulating agencies to have certain supplies and equipment. My mentor told me to ask others for help in obtaining it. She was confident that people would be happy to help me, and told me that I had to stop thinking that nobody wants to see me succeed.

She said, "You would be surprised at the number of people who are genuinely good at heart. Just go ahead and call some of these schools, and talk to them about letting you have or buy some equipment that they are not using."

Asking for help

I thought: *I wouldn't know what to say to them.*

I was embarrassed to ask for help. But I thought about our commitment to Mrs. James and the importance of what we were striving for, and realized that I had to get over this issue of pride.

I remembered what my mother did when she felt we needed something we couldn't afford while growing up. She would purchase used items from a resale shop.

I asked myself: *What did you say you were willing to do, Anna? Anything, right?*

I knew I needed to just step out on faith and do it.

So I began calling the schools.

Many of them said no, but then I found one school owner who said he was renovating his school and that I could come and get whatever I needed from them. They gave me almost everything I needed to open my doors for pennies on the dollar!

You may be accustomed to doing things all on your own, like me. Based on my past experiences, it was Preston and me against the world—and often, against the odds. But I realized that past experiences only give you past results.

You must learn to see things differently to start a business.

Lessons Learned: Keep Going and You Will Get a Yes!

- Don't let your pride keep you from success. Be willing to seek help when you know you need it. The used equipment that I was fortunate enough to find could have cost me thousands of dollars if purchased brand new. Because our funds were limited, if we had not pursued other options, our target start date could have been delayed by months.

- Do not prejudge based on past experiences. Believe in possibility and keep going.

- Don't give up. Don't stop because of a few no's. You will get a yes if you persist.

- You must be persistent in your efforts to find a way, even when you don't have the money. Not doing anything could have cost us precious time, already in short supply. It also would have cost us money; each day that went by without our doors open we lost money.

Are you a person who never asks for help, and are you proud of this because you feel strong?

But then, when you are actually in need, do you hesitate to ask for help because you don't want to come off as needy?

Are you ashamed to let others know that you are experiencing a challenge, so, instead, you decide to go it alone?

That's what I was like. I always made myself available to help others in need and it felt good to be that way. I felt blessed.

But, when you think about it, isn't it fair to give others an opportunity to bless you back?

Perhaps you have asked for help before and have been refused. Don't let that color your perspective. Clear your mind of all negative thoughts. Then believe that what you ask for will materialize. It may come from some truly unexpected places. Know that you can use the power of your magnetic mind to pull in what you want. You get what you give. Ask and you shall receive. Knock and the door will open; seek and ye shall find! It's waiting for you. Go get it!

Ask for help, not because you are weak but because you want to remain strong.

~ Les Brown

JUGGLING THROUGH THE STRUGGLE

We opened our beauty school starting with only two students. One dropped out later because she felt there weren't enough people, so we were left with one student.

As we struggled to get our business started, we started to run into financial difficulties. It was time to make some hard choices.

We understood early on that with limited income, we would experience a climate change on our journey. We just didn't know how hot the temperature would get. We only knew that we were going in anyway. And no matter what, we were willing to just put one foot in front of the other and keep going.

We needed to pay the bills for two locations: home and the business. There were two light bills, gas bills, and rent, as well as additional expenses from the business to maintain the operation. The business needed supplies, extra insurance, equipment, upkeep, and a host of other bills that seemed to keep creeping up.

It wasn't long before we had maxed out our credit cards to run the business. We couldn't buy a pair of socks on credit.

We were quickly over our heads in debt. For a while there were bill collectors calling every day. We received pink letter shut-offs every month; everybody wanted their money. The mortgage company sent us foreclosure letters every two to three months. We were always struggling and juggling the bills, trying to play catch up. I was playing the roles of more than ten people, including keeping up with my responsibilities at home.

No Turning Back

We had already made the hard decision to take everything we had and invest it into the business for the short term. We had to stay focused. No time to think about the journey or to complain, just keep going. There was no turning back now.

I prayed: *My God! How long will it take to get through this? Please don't let me fall Lord!*

I kept telling myself: *Just hold on tight! Eventually everybody is going to get paid. It will all be worth it in the end.*

I held on to the thought that this business would be life changing for us if we could just hang in there.

I took what little money we did have coming in and juggled it between the school and the home. We were on a mission.

Preston was working as much overtime as he could, and I was taking in hair clients during every spare minute.

We had to be productive every day because my family was counting on me. Preston and I knew from the start that we would have to climb some hills and that we may fall into some valleys. We had to push with everything we had. There was no turning back.

We stuck to this commitment. We paid the school bills knowing we didn't have the gas on at home. We put ourselves in a position to pay everyone off within a few years. But for now, we had to stay focused.

Lessons Learned: Keep Focused

- Be willing to go through difficulties to reach your goals.

- Stay focused on the light at the end of the tunnel at all costs. Visualize the end result every day.

- It will get better, and the struggle will be worth it.

DIFFICULT TIMES

We had many difficult times when we began our business, and I will share some of them here. Whenever you begin a new venture, you will have to climb a sharp learning curve. There will be needs that you didn't foresee and unexpected storms that you may not be prepared for. You will weather them all if you keep your focus on your goals.

The Man Is Here to Shut Off the Gas!

One day a student ran into the office and said "Mrs. Jackson, the man is here to shut off the gas!"

I gasped. A representative from the gas company had walked across the school salon floor waving a pink letter stating he was there to turn off the gas. This was in front of my clients and my students. In front of everyone.

I was ashamed and embarrassed.

I didn't want anyone to see me sweat because I was the boss. I needed to maintain a cool demeanor as though there was nothing wrong. But I felt humiliated; I knew everyone had already seen what was happening. Now everyone would know that we were in financial trouble.

My heart sank to the floor at the thought of him shutting off the gas in the middle of the day while I had clients being serviced, with hair color and chemicals that needed to be rinsed. Turning off the power meant that the hot water would be shut down. I wanted to freeze that moment in time so I could grab him and drag him out of the public's eye and into the office before he talked to anyone else.

How embarrassing! What was most distressing was that I didn't have any money and I didn't know what I was going to say. I needed to ask him to give me some time — just another week. So I pulled myself together and walked onto the clinic service floor and invited him into my office. I closed the door behind me.

The only option I had was the faith that somehow, it would all work out in my favor. I put on the humblest face and pleaded with the man not to shut off my gas.

I begged him to give me just one more day and I guaranteed the bill would be paid.

He left the office and did not shut it off that day. Thank God!

I didn't know where the money would come from but something inside of me said: *You will get that money. You made a commitment; it's on its way!* I called my brother and a few others and the bill got paid. Whew!

Lessons Learned: Think Positively

- Don't take anything personally. What we found is that most people are rooting for you to win.

- Don't assume that they are laughing at you and want you to fail. Distractions are temporary illusions standing in the way of your goal. Keep going.

- Know that there are always positive options to any problem. Creatively expose them.

If you say to yourself, *I will do whatever it takes*, then you have to mean it, even if you have to go to those who have always said no. This is not the time to be proud. For now, do what you have to, by any means necessary. This is the journey you chose to take. It builds character. You can only build muscle when you are uncomfortable. Choose to be okay with being uncomfortable while you build strength in yourself.

Strength does not come from winning. Your struggles develop your strengths. When you go through hardships and decide not to surrender, that is strength.

~ Sable Marie

Hey, Wait — That's My Car!

Sylvia, another school owner, and I were invited to a meeting that could possibly result in a contract to train students. We both needed it desperately. I drove and picked her up. We dressed as though we were already successful. We went to a Marina for a luncheon meeting.

The two men we were meeting with had begun to go over the details when the waiter came to the table to ask who was driving the white Cadillac outside. I told him that it was mine. He asked me to come with him for a moment. We all looked at each other, a little puzzled; I excused myself from the table to see what he wanted.

I followed him through the restaurant to the front door when he said, pointing out the door, "Those people are taking your car."

I looked outside and saw my car hitched up to a big red rig. I ran outside and screamed, "Hey! Wait a minute! That's my car!"

The man said, "Ma'am, I am just doing my job."

I was crying and begging him not to take the car.

He said, "Ma'am, I am so sorry but you have to call the people you leased the car from."

I thought for a moment about how he must have followed me all the way there and waited until the valet parked the car and

I went inside. I felt so embarrassed and ashamed. Tears were running down my face as I held on to the door handle and shouted for him to wait so I could get my things out of the car.

I knew we owed payments for the car but I didn't think the repossession would happen so soon. I certainly didn't think they would follow me from my home, to Sylvia's house, and then all the way downtown to get the car.

I was completely caught off guard. It was the worst timing possible. I didn't know what I was going to do next.

I stayed outside for a moment to try to pull myself together. When I walked back through the doors of the restaurant I was full of embarrassment.

I did not want to tell the restaurant manager that my car was repossessed so I told him I didn't know why they were taking it and that I knew I'd paid my bill.

I stated I would take care of this when I got home. I proceeded to go back to my table.

The two gentleman asked, "Is everything okay?"

I didn't want them to know what happened so I told them everything was fine.

I couldn't tell Sylvia while we were sitting there that we didn't have a ride home now. I didn't know how we were going to get home. But most important, I wanted to proceed with the contract negotiation. I needed this.

A few seconds later, the waiter returned to our table and looked at me. I was thinking: *Oh, no, what does he want now?*

He asked me to come with him again. Now the people at my table were really starting to wonder what was going on.

When I followed the waiter to the front desk, two policemen were standing at the desk. The manager, thinking he was being helpful, had called the police. They asked me what happened and they wanted to know if they could do anything for me. They were kind and trying to help, but the attention further embarrassed me.

I thanked them and told them I would handle it when I got home.

I returned to the table and everyone looked at me confused this time. One of the men said, "Is everything okay?"

I told him everything was fine.

And then he said, "Seriously Anna, what's going on?"

I said with a stutter after I swallowed, "They repossessed my car."

He said, "Oh! I had that happen to me—when I was about nineteen years old," he said sarcastically.

He stated that they had to leave because they had another appointment. You may have guessed that we didn't get the contract. We did find out later that the guys giving the contract lost their deal.

Meanwhile, Sylvia and I were stuck sitting there looking fine with our million-dollar outfits on, staring at the empty water glasses, trying to figure out how to get home. Sylvia eventually contacted her friend to pick us up.

When I made it home, I began looking through the newspaper to find a car that we could afford for cash. Preston and I only had two hundred dollars. We found a cheap car to drive to get us back and forth to work. It had one blue door and a pink hood with a broken latch. We had to use a clothes hanger to tie down the hood to keep it from opening and flying up as we drove.

It was not a Cadillac, but it had four wheels and a working engine. We had transportation that got the job done, at least for a short time. We had faith that it would only be needed temporarily.

Lessons Learned: Focus on the Next Step

- When you have unexpected problems, focus on the next step, instead of focusing on your feelings. In our case, first we needed a way home. After that, we needed to solve our transportation problem.

- Do not let a crisis distract you from your goal.

You will go through trials and tribulations; all new business owners experience them. But the growth you will experience will build strength that will endure even the most difficult situations.

We had to stay focused. Everything that hits you will come in the form of an illusion to distract you from your goal. You have to focus and ask for your next move. The next move may not be what you are accustomed to, but be willing to make the sacrifice if necessary to see your next step.

Be still in the moment. It could take days for your answer to come to mind but surely, in the middle of the night, or through an encounter with life, the answers will appear. They are always close to you.

Finding Gratitude in the Midst of Struggle

Our car was raggedy and the passenger door was taped shut so I had to crawl in from the driver's side in order to get in. The car had been running hot but we usually kept it filled with water and that temporarily solved the problem.

I was embarrassed by the car even though with a little extra care, it always got us where we needed to go. I told Preston to always pick me up down the street because I didn't want anyone to see me get in the car. He always picked me up so we could ride together to pick up the kids from his mother's house on the way home.

It was pouring rain one night when Preston pulled up in front of the school to pick me up from work. Needless to say, I was furious that he did that, because my students saw me crawl into that car.

I angrily asked him why he had pulled in front of the building.

He said, "I didn't want you to get wet."

Bless him. But I was still embarrassed.

As we drove away, the windshield wipers started to make a loud screeching noise as they started to drag across the window. I thought they were about to give up on us. One was working and the other was dragging.

We were in the middle of the freeway as Preston struggled to see out of the window while the big raindrops splattered heavily.

I complained to Preston, "I don't like this beat-up car. We need to find another car. I am embarrassed when you pick me up. Everyone can see how poor we are when I get in this thing. I don't like this car — it is falling further apart every day!"

In spite of the fact that it wasn't Preston's fault, and the car had actually been getting us back and forth to work for months, I continued to rant and rave.

Suddenly, the car stopped cold on us, in the middle of the freeway. I couldn't believe it.

We climbed out of the car and we walked down the freeway, up the ramp, in the dark for about a mile in the freezing-cold-pouring-down rain before we found a pay phone to call someone for help. I was crying, angry—and so regretful for speaking into existence the death of that wonderful car.

I was ashamed of myself for the way I had been behaving.

Lessons Learned: Be Grateful

- Be grateful wherever you find yourself on your journey.

- Gratitude is found even in the smallest things. That night was a wakeup call because having a car that took us from point A to point B everyday was a luxury that I had taken for granted. Having to take three busses was the only other option left. If I had to choose, I would have taken that broken down, beat-up car any day.

- We always want to have more, but here is the lesson I learned: *loving what you have brings you more.* Be grateful for what you have and recognize how far you have come.

- Don't spend time and energy on complaining. It is unproductive, unloving, and it does you no good. Stay focused; keep moving forward.

- Words are powerful and we speak life or death through them. Choose your words with Love. It will influence your outcome.

- When you awake each morning, commit to *being* the gift you want from others. This may be a simple smile or a word of encouragement.

Do you start your day feeling grumpy sometimes? Practice turning a frowning, sad person into a grateful, happy person. The gifts you will receive in return, through gratitude and love, will infuse your soul and help you to achieve a balanced mind and a happy heart.

Gratitude makes sense of our past, brings peace for today and creates a vision for tomorrow.

~ Melody Beattie

"Anna Needs to Close That Raggedy School"

Those first months were so very difficult.

Preston worked as much overtime as he could to help with the bills. The juggling between home and school became increasingly difficult for us. It was hard to stay above water. The struggle began when we were faced with eviction and utility shut offs. Our car was repossessed. I had to bring the children to work with me.

In the past, we were the ones always giving to others. When they needed money, babysitters, a ride, help in any way, Preston and I would always help in any way that we could. We felt we were independent and even when we were on welfare, we didn't ask our friends for help. But the day came that we had to put aside our pride and to reach out to others. We called on friends and family for help.

Forging Ahead Even When Others Doubt You

Unfortunately, asking for help opened us up to a great deal of criticism. In our quest, I guess we seemed desperate to some. My mother and my sister and other members of the family were worried about us.

We began to hear comments like:

Your utilities are shut off, you are about to be evicted, and you've lost your cars. You have two children, have you lost your mind?

They don't know what they are doing; Preston and Anna know nothing about how to run a business.

Nobody is going to sink their money into that bottomless pit.

Anna needs to close that raggedy school and get a job because they are losing everything.

Close that raggedy school? They didn't understand. We could not stop. We had to keep going, in spite of the naysayers.

And it's a good thing we did. Three years later, we had grown our business to over 280 students.

When we changed our mindset and started down this road, we could see clearly the possibility of success. But when we changed, the people in our world didn't know how to share our new vision or how to handle our new lifestyle.

We discovered that many of the people we knew couldn't appreciate who we were at the time because they did not know what our capabilities were. We didn't either, to begin with. It was never the business they didn't believe in; and of course they loved us. Seeing us as entrepreneurs is what they couldn't wrap their heads around.

I think it was hard for people to imagine the thought of Preston, a factory worker, and me, a kitchen helper, going from losing our jobs—and living on welfare—to owning and creating a successful business. They had only known us as regular people who worked hard and made mistakes. Of course we continued to make mistakes, but this time, it was with purpose.

When we changed our minds about who we were, we changed direction from the path we were headed in and became who we wanted to be. Our friends and family eventually began to see us as we saw ourselves: as successful business owners. We gained the respect of our family and friends, and we gained the freedom that we had planned for.

Lessons Learned: Patience and Persistence

- Be patient with friends and loved ones who don't understand your journey.

- Forge ahead with confidence even when others doubt you.

Chapter Five

Lessons We Learned in the Early Years

WHILE YOU BUILD YOUR BUSINESS

Working Another Job

The early years of a new business involve many sacrifices and the juggling of responsibilities. You will likely be trying to earn enough money to keep the business going until it is successful; this may mean that you are working another job at the same time.

If you must work another job while building your business, try to find a job that is in the field that you are seeking if at all possible, even if you can only work part-time hours. There are twenty-four hours in a day. Be flexible. Be willing to cut out time to work on your business, whether it is in developing your skills or your plan.

Schedule the time in your calendar, as if it is part of your job. It may have to be early morning or late evening if the rest of your day is busy.

You can start by doing the research needed and work up to organizing the steps to reaching your goals. You will have to prioritize to be sure that you are meeting your objectives. Whatever you put into your business, you are sure to receive back as equity.

If the job you have is not in your desired industry, create a way to start your business and build it part-time until you can replace your income. Even two hours a day devoted consistently to building the business will inch you to success. Within a year you would be much further along than if you had never started. Consistency in your practice is key.

Take Pride in Doing Your Best

I am taken aback by people who have a job, but refuse to express their full potential doing it. Perhaps, it's because they don't like their job or their boss. Arriving late, poor job performance, and not supporting the company vision all demonstrate a lack of respect.

You have been given an opportunity to earn an income. Do your best.

Experience has taught me that not to do your best at every opportunity will limit your options. You never know when someone will ask you to play at a higher level because of the experience you have gained where you are now.

Whether you are working for yourself or for another, always give it your all. Consider every job you are doing as the one you were born to do. When you change your way of thinking, you will change your attitude about work. It is no longer a job, it is part of your life, and your life is precious. Make every day of your life worth living by embracing your ambition. Even if it is working for less than you feel you are worth, remember it's just a stepping-stone. If you are known as the best at whatever you are doing, a possible new opportunity awaits you.

You may be working at a job that you don't enjoy while you are diligently working at preparing your own business. This may make you tired and impatient. Don't let it interfere with doing your job. Discipline yourself to remain a hard worker with a good attitude. Practicing this work ethic will help you succeed when you finally have your own business.

Find the Joy in All You Do

I can remember when I worked as a tray girl at a hospital. I had to set about one hundred trays in the morning before the patients received their breakfast. I went through the same process before lunch. I had to read the menu on each one and set each tray for a specific type of diet. Looking at those trays every morning seemed at first to be a boring and ominous task, but I decided that I was going to strive to be the fastest tray setter. I became so fast setting the trays that I didn't think about the monotony because it was like a game. I was so fast that I offered to set trays for others because I knew that I would be able to help them get it done fast. I just refocused my mind about the situation and it worked to my advantage. I no longer thought of it as a job, but rather as a challenge to do my best in minimal time. Just a simple task of setting trays can change the way you look at the world.

Once, when I needed to move some heavy boxes, I asked for assistance from an older man who looked like he was in good shape. He told me he worked stocking supplies at Walmart. He went on to tell me how heavy some of the boxes were, and how he challenged himself to lift more boxes than he did the last time. He went on to proudly say that he could do things many people his age could not because he consistently worked out all day.

He said, "I know people who pay to go to the gym to get these muscles and I get them free—and with a paycheck!"

Find the joy in everything you do even if it is sweeping floors or emptying garbage. Find a way to love what you do at any given moment. Trust that something is coming to you in your future that will make the experience meaningful. Do not try to figure it out now, just wait for the opportunity to present itself. Stay ready so you will not have waste time getting ready when the opportunity arises.

CHANGES THAT CAME WITH SUCCESS

As our business continued to grow, the day came that I asked Preston, "Why are we holding on to your job?"

I felt it was time for him to quit his job.

Friends, family members, and co-workers told us he would be crazy to leave a stable income, and give up the benefits and health coverage because he only had twenty years left before retiring to a lifestyle of travel and leisure. After all, that is the American Dream.

We thought: *Why hold on to a job that gives you no pleasure? And hold on to it for twenty more years?*

His health benefits were an important factor, but we could afford healthcare on our own now. Once again, we chose the road less travelled and Preston walked away from that job.

Owning our own business took extreme focus, courage, determination, and a willingness to step out of our comfort zone. We knew that we would have to commit to lifelong learning, self-development, and the changing of self-defeating past behaviors and old habits.

Was it an easy task?

No. It took belief, commitment, and persistence; and we learned as we grew. Over time, we made many mistakes and bad decisions that resulted in losses.

However, we also sat on great beaches, stayed in the finest hotels, traveled to many countries, we opened the first cosmetology school in Togo, West Africa. We lived an adventure. We enjoyed our lives and our business made millions while we built a legacy for our family.

Then it happened: Preston had a stroke at the age of forty-five. His mobility is limited as a result of the stroke.

Today, we have no regrets. We are in a state of total gratitude for the life we have because of choosing to live our lives on our own terms. Preston walking away from that job before the age of forty was the best decision we had ever made.

Sadly, the guys who worked with Preston, who tried to convince him of the importance of keeping the good job for another twenty years to maintain benefits, didn't get to see their retirement dreams come true. They all either passed away from illness, or were afflicted with a long-term disability.

We now have memories and stories to share with our grandkids. We discovered that life happens while you are on your journey to success.

Our journey was by no means over, and we had some of the most difficult challenges still ahead. You'll read more about that in the last chapter. But let's take a moment to look back on our passage to success.

What did we learn?

Oh, my, we learned so very much. We wouldn't be able to tell you everything, but I've selected twenty-five of the most important lessons we learned during the early years and give them to you below:

TWENTY-FIVE LESSONS THAT HELPED DRIVE OUR EARLY SUCCESS

1. You must be disciplined and responsible; this is your only option when you own your own business. Desperate situations that call for quick thinking will pop up, and you will be the person responsible for solving the problem.

2. Being a business owner requires making tough decisions, planning ahead, and working when you don't feel like it. You needed to be willing to exchange working 9 to 5 for working 9 a.m. to midnight. Sometimes with no salary.

3. Owning your own business takes prioritizing your schedule, doing your own marketing, advertising, researching, branding, and staying up nights until you have completed certain tasks. This may happen for quite a while, until the business is in position to hire help.

4. Life will throw you curves but you were born with the capacity to field them. It's not what happens to you, it's how you respond to it that shapes your life.

5. Don't fret too much; it will all work out. Every day you are faced with decisions to make—what to wear, where to go, who to see, what to say—and in every case, this decision will affect your future. Remember, you're making the best decision you can at the time, but you will still have options. You can change your mind if you feel it was the wrong decision.

6. Don't cling to a plan that isn't working. Set new goals and create the plan to get there. Living a life of abundance or a life of struggle are the results of the choices we make.

7. Whenever possible, if you want to be at the top of your profession, take the opportunity to update your technical skills and keep learning. Whether you have been out of school for one year or ten, it is vital that you keep your skills sharp. Everything that you learn adds value to the business.

8. *Work for what you will learn, not what you will earn* was one of the most powerful lessons I learned from reading the book, *Rich dad, Poor Dad,* by Robert Kiyosaki and Sharon Lechter. For the best education, go to work for the company you most admire. Learn the industry and the operations of running a business; see how to do things first hand. If you want to open a beauty salon, get a job in a great salon. If you want to open a coffee shop, go to work for a coffee cafe. Don't focus heavily on the pay; focus on your education. Think of it as an internship that adds value to your future goals.

9. Carve out time to work on your business, whether it is in developing your skills or your plan. If you must work a job while building your business, try to find a job that is in the field that you are seeking, even if all you can get are part-time hours. Even if you can't work in your field, make your business a priority by committing time to it every day. Make a schedule. Even if you can only afford an hour or two a day, early in the morning or late at night, keep to your commitment. Set clear objectives and take small, but consistent steps toward your goals.

10. Learn to be patient and disciplined. At times you may become annoyed with an obstacle that presents itself. Take a breather, but then go back and find your way around it, over it, or through it. Stay disciplined and steer clear of distractions. Anything that takes your eye off the prize causes you to become distracted from your journey. Having the discipline to reach your goal requires you to commit to focus regardless of what's going on elsewhere. You can easily become distracted when you carry a busy schedule. Maintain laser focus on your goal every day and add nothing else to your plate until you hit your target.

11. Who are the top ten entrepreneurs in your industry? Study what makes them successful. Study their philosophies and experiences. Plug into a community of industry professionals who are available in your area. You may not be able to approach all of the entrepreneurs you admire, but you can get into their minds by reading stories about them in books, magazines, and other periodicals. Research the web, subscribe to blogs, go to trade shows, and join trade organizations. Experts have laid the groundwork for you. There are millions of published authors who have made their ideas and knowledge available to you. Above all, read books on how to better yourself. Focus on strategies that will catapult your business and help you to grow. Many authors have placed their books in audio format, which allows you to listen while you are mobile on your phone, in the car, or even before falling asleep. This is an alternative way to gain the information and to absorb it into your consciousness.

12. Make it a habit to study for twenty minutes each day. Highlight important segments, such as statistics, history, and techniques. Apply these tips to your business.

13. Many successful entrepreneurs have videos on YouTube that you can watch for free. If your aim is to become an expert on the subject, you will need to build and develop your skills and knowledge. These are the seeds you plant within yourself to strengthen your confidence and develop your skills.

14. Motivational speakers can be inspirational, as well as being good resources for information. I am most inspired by Les Brown in his *You've Got to Be Hungry* speech; my all-time favorite books Napoleon Hill, *Think and Grow Rich*; Sharon Lecter, *Think and Grow Rich for Women*; Earl Nightingale, *The Strangest Secret*; Dr. Wayne Dyer, *Your Erroneous Zones*; Claude Bristol, *The Magic in Believing*; and *Rich Dad, Poor Dad* co-authored by Sharon Lechter and Robert Kyosaki..

15. I also loved reading about passionate visionaries such as Walt Disney, Ray Crock of McDonald's, Bernie Marcus and Arthur Blank of The Home Depot *Built from Scratch*, and other stories about journeys to business success.

16. Associations provide great settings in which you can develop beneficial relationships. If you cannot join an association, create one with a network of likeminded individuals. This can help you to share ideas, which will help you all to grow. Also connect with people in complimentary industries.

17. Always have your business cards with you. When you give them away, ask for their card in return. As soon as

you have a moment alone, write on their card a note that will help you to remember where you met and what you spoke about.

18. Build contact lists by recording every business contact you encounter.

19. Help others to build their businesses by sharing your resources, business contacts, and things you've learned. This kind of networking might seem counter-intuitive, but kindness is never wasted.

20. Steer clear of negative people and environments that can cause stress. Negativity only consumes and wastes your energy. Animosity toward others is distracting at best and destructive at worst. You can't do big things if you are distracted by small things. Maintain a positive focus and outlook on your future. Surround yourself with like-minded individuals who uplift and motivate you. Your mind and consciousness need daily positive reinforcement. Stay connected to those who bring out the best in you and vice versa. When you are positive and motivated, your light will shine so bright that you will inspire your employees, clients, and everyone you encounter.

21. When you have questions, find the answers. Think of all of the questions that are running through your mind and write them down. You will also want to research answers that will help you to stay confident in decision-making.

22. Develop your strengths. Some people are great with sports. Those who practice defining the skills that bring value to their game become the iconic figures that we look up to today.

23. Listen intently for the answers that you seek. Sometimes a person asks for advice from an expert, but then doesn't really listen to the answer because they are too busy thinking about how they will respond. They already know what the experts say; in fact, they may even know what you are going to say next; their minds are so full that they have no capacity to learn. It reminds me of this phrase: *The mind is like a parachute; it only works when it's open.* Open your mind and listen.

24. Take the time to recognize when you are talking too much and practice conscious listening. If you are listening to someone who is experienced and successful, give them the respect that they have earned from their accomplishments. They may reveal a clever strategy, and you will recognize it if you listen carefully.

25. Choose your words wisely before you speak. You can never take them back once they leave your lips. If you let them fly without having thought about them first, you may regret it for a lifetime.

Chapter Six

Setting Goals and Committing to Your Venture

DO YOU HAVE A VISION?

When someone told me about goal setting years ago, I had certainly heard it before. For many years it seemed that at every conference, seminar, and class I had taken relating to success. Everyone said the same thing: *Set a goal.*

The most important benefit of setting goals isn't achieving your goal. It's what you do and the person you become in order to achieve your goal; that's the real benefit.

~ Jim Rohn

I have taken dozens of courses, listened to hundreds of audiotapes and listened to countless interviews with successful people. I've read hundreds of books. I've paid thousands of dollars to learn from some of the greatest personal development gurus in the country.

When it came to goal setting, they were all saying the same thing: *Have a vision.*

Write your goals down; carry them in your pocket. Say it over and over throughout the day. Plan for three months, six months, one year, five years, and ten years. You've probably heard similar advice over and over again; there is nothing new on the subject. Those words are solid and have proven results consistently.

We continue to hear testimonials from those who have used these principles and created success in their business.

DO YOU HAVE A PLAN OF ACTION?

Marvin listened to the testimonials of several speakers who talked about their circumstance prior to becoming a success. While listening to many of their stories, he became tearful.

When the session was over, he said with enthusiasm and confidence, "With the education I have acquired over the years, and the resources I know that I can tap into, I can surely do what they did and better!"

He was excited and was eager to get home to put his plan on paper because he knew exactly how he would execute it. After a week went by, I asked him how he was coming with his plan. He stated that he was still excited and working on a few things and he wanted to take his time and really think his strategy through.

A month went by, and then a year. Marvin never made his big move. He never created a plan of action. Life got in the way and over time, nothing happened. He said he felt stuck in his present circumstance.

Sadly, Marvin is not alone; many can relate to this experience. Having small children, a health issue, a negative spouse, feeling hostage to a job and its benefits are all good reasons to be stuck, but they are obstacles that can be overcome.

Without a goal or a plan of action, the possibility of achieving a better life is not within reach. You must prepare in advance.

Setting goals and achieving them becomes a systematic approach. They are like a compass, they point you in the direction you are heading and keep you on course. Having goals forces you to stretch beyond your comfort zone into a place of competence and confidence. But first you must take baby steps to begin.

Preston and I had to first get rid of some of the habits and belief systems that were ingrained inside us.

In some cases, we did the opposite of what others did to reach success. Not everyone would make the decision NOT to pay their bills, for instance. It was a risk, not unlike the risk that Robert Townsend took when he made his first film on credit using his American Express card. By the time the bill was due; he had sold his film and paid the bill from the proceeds.

Your daily habits are created by your daily decisions moment by moment. Those decisions have created your level of success as it stands today.

Are you happy with that level of success?

If it is not what you want, the good news is that you get to change it. Part of professional growth is change. You must develop new habits. Believe that you can create a better outcome by setting your intentions and acting on them.

It is said that it takes around thirty days to design and frame a habit.

Can you commit thirty days to form habits for success? Small changes create huge results. Build on what's working, and change what is not. It's as simple as that.

What habits will you change?

ARE YOU STANDING IN YOUR OWN WAY?

Analysis Paralysis

Stanley was a hairstylist who worked in a beauty salon. He had a desire to work for himself, so he started a small boutique selling clothing in the small space of a flea market. It wasn't what he really wanted to do but it brought in a little extra income. His passion was being a hairstylist. He said he wanted to learn everything he could about the business, so he could someday open a salon of his own. This was his dream.

He enrolled into the local college to take business classes, and would attend every seminar he heard about. He constantly gave advice and voiced his opinions about business to others. Although his dream was to open a salon, Stanley still wanted to make sure that he was ready because he did not want his business to fail.

A business owner who ran a popular salon made the decision to retire and sell. She offered the option to Stanley to take the business over. She had a great existing clientele located in a very profitable area. Stanley saw this was an amazing opportunity, and it was just what he was looking for. He knew that this building would sell fast if others got word of it, so he negotiated a deal with her and quickly secured the building for his new venture.

Stanley still wanted to continue income-generating at the other salon, so he decided he would wait to open the new salon in the upcoming months because he needed to adjust his clients to the change of location. He waited to make sure everything was perfect.

Current clients of the former owner knocked on the door repeatedly but there was no answer. Hairstylists and nail techs asked him for applications to work in his new salon. But he declined. The doors remained closed.

Stanley was very skeptical about opening the salon or hiring on new people. He wanted to find just the right people. The problem was he never searched for those people. He continued to work his day job, holding on to the building until he felt the time was right.

When other business owners tried to advise him, he couldn't hear them. He continued to lose money every day. Stanley said he needed to get a system in place so that his employees could be properly oriented and everything would work well. He paid the rent on the building each month while telling people he would open the salon when it was ready.

Stanley never opened the salon doors. With the costs of rent and other associated expenses, including utilities, he ran out of money fast and had to let the building go. He also took a big loss on his existing small businesses because he did not focus on any one thing. He was spread too thin.

He eventually let go of everything and went to work on a nine-to-five job. In the end, he said he finally felt relieved; like he could breathe again when it was all over.

Making that initial start is difficult for everyone, but it will never happen if you allow yourself to be a victim of analysis paralysis.

Is this your tendency?

Are you constantly on the search for more details, navigating every search engine, and taking every class?

Do you search deeper and deeper and never actually get to the starting gate for fear of failure?

To keep yourself from this kind of paralysis, set a deadline to get started. Prioritize, get your most important questions answered by that date, and move forward.

Don't Let Fear Keep You From Committing to a Venture

Do you want to start your own business, but every day, you go to work for someone else instead because you are afraid to take the risk?

That job that you have is proof that owning your own business is possible. You prove it to yourself every time you punch in. You are an employee for a business that somebody else took a risk to start. Your boss saw an opportunity, made the decision to invest in that opportunity, and built a business.

Perhaps you try to rationalize your choice.

You think: *I have a family to feed and bills to pay.*

You feel trapped in an endless cycle and you feel that you have no other option.

You are filled with fear of the unknown:

- Fear of failing
- Fear of taking a risk
- Fear of winning and then losing it all.

What if you try it and it doesn't work out?

You think: *I won't be able to go back to my old life. I won't have my old job to fall back on.*

We almost fell into this trap ourselves. When Preston and I were struggling after we lost our jobs and had to turn to welfare, I knew I wanted us to start a business of our own. But when Preston got his job back, life went back to normal. We put the business idea on hold and went back to a lifestyle that we didn't enjoy.

I am grateful that we woke up and decided to make the move necessary to start our business.

You may be waiting until you have a secure enough back-up plan. This is your fear talking. If you are wrapped up in fear, it is likely you will never feel secure enough to take the risk.

Keep in mind that your life right now may not be as secure as you think. Consider what happened to us before we started our business — even though we had stayed locked into our so-called stable lifestyle, keeping what everyone around us considered *good* jobs, we ended up on welfare.

Well, we can go on forever talking about what holds us back, but I know the reason you are reading this book is because you are ready to move forward with your own ideas. Let's get to it!

Lessons Learned: Stop Overthinking

- Stop over-thinking. If you make a decision that does not work for you, it's okay. You get to learn from it. You can always fix it. But if you make no decision, you get nothing.

- You will start your business with what you know. The learning curve will be sharp in the beginning; you will find out just how much you *don't* know as you get started. Be ready to learn and adapt; it will be a wonderful life experience.

- Fear is natural. Learn to use it to propel you into action. Think about a running back on a football field. When he catches the ball, he may fear he won't make it to the end zone. But he tucks the ball in under his ribs anyway, and runs toward the goal, hell-bent on scoring. He knows he will be met with obstacles along the way; the defensive lineman who will do everything in their power to stop him, but what would happen if he didn't try? Running toward the goal is the mission of both a good running back and a good entrepreneur; it is in that mission that the path to greatness is laid.

You don't have to be great to start, but you have to start to be great.
~ Zig Ziglar

Chapter Seven

Business Plans and Preparation

ONE STEP AT A TIME

You have read the previous sections of this book in order to learn about how to develop the entrepreneurial mindset, and understand the challenges and benefits of becoming a successful business owner. Now it is time to begin.

Before you actually open your doors for business, there are many preparations you will need to make. From researching accountants to filling out licensing applications to planning a budget, the many tasks involved with beginning a business can be overwhelming; just take it one step at a time.

Commit to your path and spend time — every day — moving toward your goal.

SELECT A GOOD BUSINESS IDEA

Let's begin by choosing the right idea to start. It is likely that you have a list of ideas to choose from. Where do you begin?

How do you get going on the right path?

Don't Overthink

When Preston and I built our business, it was without a formal education, without computers, Google, smartphones, without all the other technology and resources that are available today. Yet we were able to create a seven-figure business within three years.

As you have read already, it took a while for us to adopt the mindset we needed, but once we had decided that we were going to start a business, we just picked the field we wanted and selected how we wanted to proceed. We didn't overthink the situation.

Overthinking may be more difficult to avoid in the current information age. We have so many resources now for finding information. This information windfall can be helpful, but it can also be a hindrance. It is far too easy to succumb to information overload which will put you in a state of confusion and indecision.

Are you prone to overthinking? Information overload may be particularly difficult for you.

As I said, we didn't overthink the situation. We took a step and then took another. When we got into a bind, we figured it out and kept going.

Many mom-and-pop businesses started this way. They didn't necessarily know the direction they were going in, and they didn't have a lifeline to pull them through. They just kept going in the way they thought it would work; perhaps, they even received some guidance along the way.

We didn't reinvent the wheel with newfound ideas. We followed success principles that we found in books and tapes. We studied the minds of successful people. We watched, listened, attended lectures, and implemented the knowledge we acquired.

We found success models and we picked and chose the ideas we could best grow from, to tweak to our particular business idea. We duplicated their efforts, and duplicated their success. It was simple math. Well, maybe not exactly simple, but the principles date back generations. If you want to get what someone has, be willing to do what they did.

Just Pick One

It is likely that you have many choices and may have difficulty selecting the right idea, or the right route to success.

With so many ideas to choose from, you may be wondering: *how do I choose?*

Don't follow every new lead that comes up; you will become more and more confused. It has been proven that *confused people do nothing*. Eliminate confusion. Just choose a direction to go in and allow the lesson to begin. You can always go back and make adjustments later.

Of all of the ideas you thought up, choose one business project that you would like to start with. It is best to begin by focusing on only one major idea to build your business from. Don't worry about the other ideas you have; you will get to the ones you want in time.

You might be tempted to start several projects at once. Resist the temptation; you will spread yourself too thin and this will cause you to get distracted along the way. Instead, give each project a laser-sharp focus. You will appreciate the journey more and give each project thereafter the attention it deserves.

How do you know which idea to choose and which project to begin first? You must be true to your vision, but must also consider your timetable and prerequisites. For example, if you are short on cash, when you are sorting through your ideas, you may want to choose one that will make the most money in the short term.

Have you already selected an idea? How do you determine if it is a good idea? How can you tell if it will bring you fulfillment? How do you know if it is financially viable?

Ask yourself these four questions:

1. Can your business idea solve a problem?

2. Can it help someone?

3. Are you passionate about this idea?

4. Have you envisioned a way to pay the bills?

If you are able to answer these questions positively, with confidence, then you are probably on the right track.

Business Idea Suggestions

If you are just beginning to consider starting a business, but haven't yet chosen a project, read through these hints:

- Do you enjoy talking and helping people? Perhaps you may want to be a speaker, a presenter, motivator, consultant, comedian, or a realtor.

- Are you retired from working many years in a particular industry? What part of the job did you enjoy? Perhaps you can capitalize on that by providing that service. Did you learn something that you could possibly package into a consulting opportunity? Writer, editor, billing, home care provider are a few suggestions.

- Are you detailed? Can you pull a skill from your experience that could create your business? If you are a legal secretary or paralegal, you can prepare legal forms and demonstrate how to complete them. If you work in an accounting department, you can provide assistance with tax forms.

- The hot new thing nowadays is to be the *virtual assistant*. You can choose to do anything you are particularly skilled at. There are websites where you can find freelancing work doing administrative duties. Also Fiverr and Upwork are great sites to showcase your services and make money too. If you are an organized individual, people need you in their lives to organize their documents, their kitchens, even their closets.

- Do you like to help people? Do you find yourself wanting to assist others? You may want to look into something like the medical profession where you can assist others on-call, or set up an online service that would allow you to assist many people through virtual technology and outsourcing.

- Do you enjoy teaching? If you have some expertise, you can be a tutor or a music instructor.

- Are you trained in healthcare? You might consider the home healthcare industry, providing transportation to medical appointments, in-home care if you are a trained nurse, or counseling sessions in the home if you are a certified therapist.

- Do you love animals? What about starting your own dog-sitting, walking or grooming business? So many people work long hours and are away from their pets for many hours each day. They would love to know someone who could step into the void and provide companionship—and much needed relief—to their pets.

- Are you active? What about applying at a cruise line? Provide dance or cooking lessons? If you love exercise, provide an exercise class out of your home or become a personal trainer. People love to have someone cheering them on and coaching them. They get their desired results faster.

- Are you creative or like to sell? If you love creating original artwork or jewelry, maybe an *Etsy* store would work for you. Earning money on eBay can be low on startup costs and you can start with the household goods you already own.

- Network marketing is a great way to make income while you build a business. I can testify to the fact that network marketing works because I have personally experienced success on many levels as a distributor. Network marketing allows you to build your strength and skills in many ways. Most important, it can help you become an expert on developing and maintaining a business network.

- Are you interested in the beauty industry? There is a huge array of opportunities to choose from. You can become the specialist in one area of expertise, a platform artist, consultant, analyst, you can rent a chair, start a business by renting a suite to sublease several chairs to others, make straight profit just cutting hair, become a celebrity stylist, or do service calls in nursing homes, assisted living facilities, or similar venues. You can also provide a service for special occasions such as weddings, proms, children's parties, spa parties, makeup and nails, and makeovers.

CREATE A PLAN OF EXECUTION

Once you have chosen your first project, be crystal clear about your intentions:

1. What is your goal?

2. What steps do you need to take?

3. What is your deadline?

Create a *plan of execution*. This is the series of steps that you intend to take in order to achieve your goals. Write your plan on paper. You might be tempted to skip this step, but it is absolutely necessary. This isn't something you can just talk into action. When you write down your plan, you make it clear—to yourself—what you want to happen and how you intend to do it.

Stating your business plans clearly will help you to lay out the direction in which you are taking your business. Detail all associated operations for efficiency and flow.

From your plan of execution, create a *plan of daily actionable steps* toward achieving your goal. Breaking down the steps into smaller sections will allow you to achieve mini goals on the way to reaching your ultimate goal.

Having manageable steps will allow you to build your confidence while getting ready for the next phase. This process will give you opportunities to see incremental accomplishments—for which you can pat yourself on the back — that will help keep you focused on your path.

Set Goal Dates

Set a deadline for each goal and *write it down*. Writing it down makes it official.

- You will be able to prioritize your time by conquering difficult tasks with laser focus and getting the job done by the deadline, even if you have to stay up all night to get it done without the many distractions that eat up valuable time.

- When you attended school, it was important for you to read the novel and complete a book report by a deadline. Knowing the importance of it drove you to finish it on time because you knew the consequences if you didn't. Think about how you felt when the assignment was completed. How gratifying was it when you turned in your assignment, when you were rewarded with a good grade, or praised for hard work because you knew you did your best? Nothing has changed. Continue to do your best in reaching your deadline.

- Setting a deadline is the most important aspect of setting goals. It helps to ensure that you will get it done. Like they say: *A dream without a deadline is just a dream.*

Managing Your Time

Time management is a vital skill for a business owner.

Are you someone who is always busy, and never has enough time? On the surface, it seems as though you are doing everything.

You are exhausted by the thought of it, but at the end of the day ask yourself this, did you really get the most important, impactful tasks done? Or was your time and energy nonproductive?

Sometimes we are so busy doing nothing that we don't have time to do anything important.

Create a way to prioritize, and to consistently execute tasks on your list. A friend taught me a method for time management. It works for me. It may seem complicated for some, but you can design your own version. Try it and see what you think:

- At the beginning of the week, make a list of everything that needs to get done.

- Categorize the list by the activity necessary to get it done. For example; C might indicate calls, M meetings, and W writing and reviewing.

- Decide on the amount of time you will commit to each category and schedule a time. Calls, for instance might be scheduled between 9:00 and 9:30 a.m.

- Place this information on your weekly calendar, spreading out the tasks appropriately over the week. This is your plan and the tasks you must tackle this week.

- Start each day with your calendar and make a commitment to knock those tasks off your calendar each day. At the end of the day, you will feel like you have accomplished something.

Take time and put forth the effort and energy needed to establish exactly what is required when creating your plan of action. This may take you a few hours or weeks. Every goal is different but each will demand time to plan. Think each goal through.

Create a list of tasks that will move you to action. Do not confuse a checklist with activity. A checklist is necessary, but it's just a list. You must take action to accomplish the tasks. That is the only way to produce the results you seek.

When you create your lists of tasks, it should include how and when each task will be completed. A checklist names the tasks as items in a list, but getting specific by making a *task schedule* will help move you to action. What is the difference?

Here is an example of a checklist:

- ☐ Start business
- ☐ Get license application
- ☐ Create a flyer
- ☐ Website designers
- ☐ Look for marketing books
- ☐ Read three books

A list like this could sit on a desk forever if you do not set activities and deadlines into motion.

In contrast, look at this task schedule:

Daily: (*Read*) I will read books that are relevant to my industry every morning at 7:00 for a minimum of thirty minutes.

Monday: (*Go*)

9:00

- ☐ Office Supply
- ☐ Insurance
- ☐ Sam's Club

☐ Bank—set up acct

☐ State auction—equipment

☐ Car tune-up

☐ Grocery store

Tuesday: (*Review/Call*)

9:00–10:00

☐ Review: requirements for license

☐ Check cosmetology state laws

10:30

☐ Calls: Adrian about the book

☐ Publishing co. re: book order

☐ Mickey in accounting

☐ B&B Marketing to confirm meeting

Wednesday: (*Review/Write*)

9:00–2:00

☐ Complete licensing application

☐ Research comparisons of ABC, Do-Re-Mi companies

☐ Pull and review regulations

3:00

☐ Deadline for exhibits

Thursday: (*Calls*)

9:00

☐ Calls: Adam re: website design

☐ Lisa — confirm lunch

☐ Terry — insurance set up

☐ State — send requirements

Friday: (*Meet*)

11:00

☐ BB Marketing — social media campaign

1:00

☐ Star Graphics — see logo samples

3:00

☐ Attorney — set up corporate structure

To merely say that you want to open a business isn't enough. Without a schedule of activities or tasks to carry it out, you won't get it done. But if you put the list of items into your calendar, along with specific end-dates, you will get the ball rolling. You *will* get it done.

Employ some kind of management system that can help you to coordinate your day. Creating your list at the beginning of the week for the entire week helps you to stay on track. Review the list each day for updates as necessary to maintain a clear focus. When you have a planned schedule, it is hard to steer away from the tasks to be done before the day is over.

Who wants to add to tomorrow what you could have finished today? Don't add it to the next day or week. Small tasks done consistently each day will ensure you to stay on course without becoming overwhelmed. You can do it.

Now you are actively working toward your goal, not just reading and writing.

Time is the most precious commodity we have on earth. But very few of us know it. Everything else can be replaced — except life. But time can never be copied. So the question becomes, how are you using the most valuable asset on earth? You only have so much, you know. Are you spending it trying to better yourself and others? Building something that will outlast you? Making sure your name and memory will be recorded in a positive light? Or are you wasting time on things that don't matter? TV, gossip, downing others who are doing the things you refuse to commit to? Choose wisely because the clock is ticking and time waits for no one. Also, know that some opportunities in life are time sensitive, meaning you only have a limited amount of time to act on them.

~ Chauncey Joiner

PRELIMINARY MARKETING TASKS

Market Research

Research the market to determine the need for your particular idea, comparing your idea to similar ideas in the market.

- Don't reinvent the wheel. You can find a model that you can work with that will save you many days and hours of thought and sweat.

- Learn and become inspired by those who have already laid the groundwork for you. Tweak it to fit your particular idea.

- Many people feel gratified in knowing that they have an original idea, this is great if you are a Thomas Edison, but for most of us, we could simply use our ideas and our genius to make an already existing product better, or use the same model idea to create something different.

- Be careful to look for models that work. If they are not doing well, what can you do to make them better? There is always an opportunity to turn lemons into lemonade.

- Look up state laws and regulations that govern your business, including license requirements.

- Organize all of your research material carefully so you have answers at your fingertips once you begin your business.

Improve Your Computer Skills

Are you in a business in which computer use is important? It is hard to imagine a business for which you would answer *no*. Make an effort to learn and improve computer skills that are useful for your business.

Stay abreast of new technology. We become antiquated when we refuse to learn. Many of us don't want to keep up with the rapid growth of technology. You can't keep up with everything but it is vital that you keep up with what's important to the survival of your business. Don't become a dinosaur. They're extinct!

A few ideas are listed below:

- Get comfortable with using the Internet, email, and social media.

- Learn how to use Excel for spreadsheets to keep track of records.

- Learn how to use accounting software to keep track of your credits and debits.

- Make your own templates to do things faster and more efficiently.

Build Your Online Presence

- Social media platforms allow you to become exposed to markets on an international scale. Having a professional website and logo and being connected to the many platforms that are available will allow you to enter markets you may not know exist.

- When someone wants to know about your business, the first response is usually to look you up online. The online presence, for many consumers, represents your company's official capacity for conducting business.

- Start to build your *brand identity* online. A brand identity tells the public about the focus of your business as well as the style and personality of your company. Anything you send or give to others with regard to your business should always be representative of your business model and brand including business cards, letterhead, letters, marketing, and advertising.

BEGIN TO CREATE YOUR CORPORATE STRUCTURE

Your corporate structure will vary with the kind of business you are starting. No matter what you will be doing, an accountant and an attorney will be vital to your business, and you should begin to build your relationships with them before you open your doors.

Contact an Accountant

If you are starting small, you can hire an accountant to help you set up a system of bookkeeping that you can manage yourself until you are ready to hire someone full-time. You will want to know important information you will need for filing your taxes at the end of the year.

Contact an Attorney

Hire an attorney to advise you on the best way to set up your corporate structure for your particular business. He will also inform you of other particulars necessary for business start-ups.

You will want to interview several attorneys and accountants to be sure they are meeting your particular needs. You will read more about this in the next chapter.

FINANCING YOUR BUSINESS

Now that you've decided to start your business, you may be a little nervous.

Who's going to pay the bills?

First things first: take a deep breath. I will give you some ideas about creative financing, such as how to save money and cut costs. After all, you are starting your own business to make money.

Balancing Business and Income Needs

It may be best to start out small. You don't want to quit your job only to rack up debt you may have a hard time paying back. Remember, this is your dream; don't sabotage it by getting into debt right away.

Instead, your job can function as your business loan until you can replace your income. Make a schedule that allows you some time to work on your business. A few options are given below.

- Perhaps you can work a regular job for three or four days a week, and commit your free days to your business. Stay focused. Trying to work at home can be challenging. You will notice that there is laundry piling up, and it will be hard to stay away from it. You will see that you're running low on milk and think that maybe you can take a break to go grocery shopping. Set a time schedule and stick to it. Establish a work area and keep yourself in it for an appointed duration. Set yourself deadlines for each project you want to complete.

- If you aren't ready to work part-time, work full-time for a set period, telling yourself that you'll save one day of pay each paycheck toward your business. Put that money aside until you have enough to work part-time.

- Another option is to become a freelancer. Do what you do now, only set it up as a business from home or freelance. Outsource your freelancing services to your prior employer. If you were an exemplary employee, with a good reputation, then they should be happy to give you work. Sometimes it seems like freelancers get more per hour, but actually, it is cheaper for a company to hire them because they don't need to give them benefits such as vacation pay, health benefits, etc.

Options for Financing

If you need to obtain financing because of equipment needed for your business, for example, here are some ideas for financing your business.

1. **Small Business Administration (SBA) Loans:**

    Under the various loan programs of the SBA, you can borrow money for a variety of business purposes, including adding to working capital, purchasing inventory or equipment, refinancing other debts, buying real estate, or even financing the acquisition of other businesses.

2. **Crowd Funding:**

    Crowdfunding is the process of raising money to fund a project or business venture from donors using an online platform, such as *Kickstarter, Indiegogo,* and *Crowdfunder.*

3. **Credit Cards:**

    Using credit cards allows you leverage when starting out, but only use this option if absolutely needed and pay the debt off as quickly as possible from the profits earned from your business. And be careful; you don't want to finance your business with 22 percent interest. Look for cards with an introductory offer — perhaps with no interest for the first six months or more. This should get you going and you'll be able to pay it off quickly.

4. **Home Equity Loan or Line of Credit:**

    If you own a home, you can check with your bank about the possibility of obtaining either a home equity loan or a home equity line of credit.

5. **Investors:**

    Do you know anyone who would be interested in putting some money into your business? You can offer them a share in the business with a return for their money. This can be a match made in heaven.

CREATIVE BUDGETING TIPS FOR NEW ENTREPRENEURS

How can you minimize your start-up costs?

Here are some ideas:

1. **Establish a Home Office:**

    Today, with a computer, printer, phone, and Internet, you can easily do business from home with little capital. According to Study Trends, more than 69 percent of U.S. entrepreneurs start their business from home, keeping the costs at a minimum. Not only will you be able to work in your pajamas with a cup of coffee beside you, you can also get a tax write-off. Many people are avoiding the added expense of a brick-and-mortar building. Amongst the list of garage starters are: Steve Jobs, Bill Gates, Google, Mattel, HP, Disney, Amazon, and Harley Davidson. Go to the library or café to use the Internet; they are also convenient places for meetings. Many places now have shared, co-working office space where self-employed or mobile folks can share space for a small fee.

2. **Use Your Skills:**

    Start a business that uses your current skills, talent, or experience to start your business. This will allow you to start where you are in business without any added expense. You can capitalize on helping others grow with the skills they don't have and you do.

3. **Avoid Random Spending:**

   Small daily expenditures add up. Make your coffee at home and take your lunch to work with you.

4. **Purchase Equipment at a Discount:**

   Check out garage sales, auctions, or wholesalers. Don't be too shy to ask other people in your industry if they have used equipment you can purchase; you may be able to obtain it at a fraction of the price.

5. **Dumpster Diving:**

   An actress friend of mine tells how her director was in the back of a hotel in Las Vegas when he saw the staff throwing away the set of the *Lion King*. He could see how valuable those props could be for his upcoming stage shows. So he and a few of his buddies went dumpster diving and retrieved all of the sets for future stage productions. Always ask permission before you do this, of course.

6. **Use Free Social Media:**

   Get the word out about your business using sources of free media. Use word-of-mouth advertising, attend social gatherings and events, use free social media on the Internet, optimize all networking opportunities, and establish yourself in the online marketplace.

7. **Create a Website for Free:**

   Having a website is a necessary part of doing business these days. It is not an option. One of the first references an individual may use to validate an official business is to ask for website information. This is also how most new customers, looking for your particular services, will find you. With the free sites now available, there is just no excuse not to have a website. There are many great website builders — wix.com, for example — and you don't need to know anything about programming to use them. You can use a template to create a beautiful and effective website.

8. Advertise With Business Cards:

Business cards are inexpensive; many companies on the web provide the first two hundred free. That is plenty to get you started. Pass them to everyone whenever you see a networking opportunity.

9. Consider Outsourcing Affordable Services:

Use freelancers so you can pay as you go without making a commitment. Don't know how to optimize the search engine for your website? Try hiring someone from your prior company's computer service department to do this as a freelancer. Have your logo, graphics, fliers, and business cards created by freelancers working via companies such as Fiverr, Elance, Upworks, and Pro, to name a few.

10. Barter Whenever Possible:

Help someone else to develop their business in exchange for them helping you. Giving and receiving is a win-win opportunity. Do you love photos in an album but don't have the time or patience to scrapbook? Perhaps you can provide a service in exchange for this. Perhaps you have a window-washing service and need childcare services. You can barter childcare for window washing.

Chapter Eight

Build Your Success Team

A PROFESSIONAL TEAM

Running a business can be rewarding but it is challenging at times. This is why choosing the right business advisors will add value to your company and assist with your vision. It is essential that you partner with a professional team.

Your team should include an accountant, a lawyer, professional contractors, bankers, and business managers when necessary. Align yourself with skilled professionals; hire the best you can afford, not the cheapest. Create positive relationships that will feed your mind with encouragement and knowledge, and with mentors who know more about the business industry than you do.

When choosing the team, you want to know that you are working with experienced professionals who are active in their profession's organizations. You want professionals who can plan with you and give ideas and advice throughout the year to help you achieve better outcomes. Consider asking for referrals from successful industry professionals.

ATTORNEYS AND ACCOUNTANTS

Because your business is vital to you, it is important that you work with an experienced attorney and accountant who are familiar with your profession and can advise you based on the laws that regulate your industry. Hiring attorneys and accountants who say they can do anything for anyone is not the best approach.

There are distinct advantages to hiring a specialist, someone who has worked with your industry as a niche market:

- You won't have to explain to them the importance of your particular issue or concern because they will have already handled that problem many times.

- They will be well aware of your specific business needs.

- They can advise you on the best way to handle any given situation based on their experience working with other clients in your industry.

- You will feel confident knowing that when you are presented with forms and documents to be signed, they will have been well thought out for your particular business.

- A good attorney will be able to assist you in setting up your business, expanding your business, contract negotiations, lease agreements, and legal issues.

- If your attorney has to go to battle for you in court, an experienced professional will serve the best interests of your company.

- An accountant who has worked in your industry will have the expertise and the experience to represent your tax concerns and pull you through an audit if necessary.

- It is important that all professionals stay updated on the latest information when it pertains to taxes and accounting. The government provides hundreds of tax breaks that can be written off that are beneficial to you. You want to be sure that the accountant knows how to advise you throughout the year so that you can take advantage of all tax breaks that are due to you.

This is not the place to cut corners. Don't be motivated by the cheapest rate, you will want to know that you are working with those who can offer you the best advice which means better results.

Hiring an Accountant

If you don't choose wisely, you risk losing a lot of money when filing your taxes, or worse, you could face stiff penalties. Tax evasion is illegal; be sure to file your taxes on time. Interview several accountants or attorneys before making a selection. You need to ask questions and tell them what you expect from them. Consider the following guidelines when hiring an accountant:

- Explain what is crucial to your business.

- Ask for a monthly review of your records.

- Request a regular face-to-face or conference call meeting for updates.

- Learn how to read a financial statement.

- Know when you are profiting or losing so you can improve your financial situation before the year ends.

- When you are just starting out, you may want to maintain your own records to keep expenses down, but you should still obtain an accountant's advice in setting up your recordkeeping system. This way, as you grow, turning the operations over to an accounting firm and bookkeeper will be smooth and less costly.

Attorneys as Advisors

Your attorneys will provide you with advice and counseling for any problem that involves a legal issue. The law can be complex, and a good attorney can help you understand your options as well as the consequences of any actions that you may be considering.

We once tried to help someone applying for jobs by referring her to another school district looking to hire teachers. We told her the salary offer they had stated to us. She applied and got the job. For some reason, the salary they paid her was less than the amount they had advertised to us. After weeks of her complaining to us, we paid her the difference as a courtesy. Our attorney told us that our decision to pay her was overkill because she was not our employee.

Although she stayed on and did not quit the job, we received a summons and complaint that she wanted to sue us, not the people she actually worked for.

Because we had established an attorney-client relationship with a large corporate firm, we called them and we were advised over the phone how we should proceed. The fees would have been very high if they went to court to represent us, but from our conversation, we were able to make a decision on how best to go forward.

We decided to represent ourselves in this case—although if this were a case of negligence or other liability, we certainly would have had our attorney represent us. We took all of the documentation our lawyer helped us create and the judge ruled in our favor. Having an attorney to represent us in other cases has saved us thousands of dollars that would have been awarded to the other side.

Lessons Learned: Ask for Professional Advice

- Always consult with your attorney on issues you do not understand.

- Ask for advice for any problem that may have a legal impact.

- Lead with your head, not with your heart, when it comes to your business. Be compassionate, but keep personal affairs outside of the business arena.

NOT CHOOSING A GOOD ACCOUNTANT COST US DEARLY

We hired an accountant to maintain our books.

He told us, "You should not have to focus on the accounting; that's what you hired me for."

Beware whenever you hear those kinds of words!

We trusted that he would advise us well on our accounting and tell us what we should do. We believed if we were doing something wrong he would alert us in a timely manner so that we could always be in compliance. We wanted him to help us maintain good records, file our taxes on time, and perform necessary audits. This was what we explained to him first when we hired him.

In the beginning, he told us he would come to see us on a monthly basis and go over the finances. He would catch us up on all of the previous months that were not done and he would always let us know where we stood at any given time. That is not what happened.

He did not come into our office regularly. When he did, he would be there for about ten minutes and leave. He never appeared to catch up and always stated that he would work it out as soon as he finished something else. He always came regularly for his payment, however.

We didn't understand the accounting jargon so we just let him do what he did best: Lie! I was so busy working on other parts of our business that I didn't think about the importance of investigating how the accounting was working. I didn't think it was necessary.

I admit I didn't know a lot about accounting and that was part of the reason I stayed away from it. That's why I hired a professional to do the accounting; so I wouldn't have to worry about that side of the business. My field was cosmetology. Back then, we didn't take the time to learn even basic accounting. Big mistake.

During tax season, we ended up paying the government thousands upon thousands of dollars when we filed our taxes because we were not properly counseled on what we could have done to avoid this heavy expense. We could have purchased equipment, supplies and a host of other tax write-offs that would have benefited our business, but by the beginning of the next year, it was too late.

It's not that we didn't want to pay our fair share of taxes, but smart business owners know how to work within the tax system to benefit their business. The government allows you to legally engage in tax avoidance by taking advantage of tax deductions and tax credits that are offered. There are so many creative ways that you can avoid paying too much tax but you have to do it within the tax year. Now it was too late.

Imagine my frustration. I was furious. I didn't want to admit it but realistically, I knew it was really my fault. I should have never given him full control without following up regularly. I knew better; I was always taught to *inspect what you expect.*

What did we do? We fired him.

Although we lost money, we learned a lot by going through this troublesome time.

We knew exactly what to look for when seeking another accountant. We knew the right questions to ask. We interviewed many accountants before finding the one we were comfortable with.

We knew now we needed to see the numbers on a regular basis and at-will, so we hired someone who used a program that we could navigate ourselves to review our expense reports. Using this software, we could see if we were hitting our targeted goals without even calling the accountant.

For that entire next year, we followed up weekly either on a conference call or in person.

The new accountant not only helped us to understand our accounting, but he also took the time to advise us regularly on what we needed to do when he thought our spending was not aligning with our goals.

Lessons Learned: Keep Your Eye on the Business

- You are in business to make money not lose it. Stay on target.

- In all areas of your business, hire quality professionals you can trust, but check in with them frequently.

- A person in business is not expected to be an expert in every area, but each business owner should have a basic knowledge of laws affecting the business.

This was a costly education, but a huge opportunity for growth. We had hands-on experience that taught us lessons that we could take with us for the rest of our business career.

FIFTEEN GOOD ACCOUNTING TIPS

1. Hire someone who is familiar and experienced with the finances in your industry.

2. Interview several accountants before you make a decision.

3. Never allow anyone to have total control of your finances without your regular input.

4. Take the time to learn the basics of accounting so you will know what is going on with your finances regularly.

5. It is critical that you learn how to read a balance sheet. Review your balance sheet yourself each month and ask pertinent questions about it.

6. Pay special attention to the categories the expenses are put into. This happens when the accountant is not sure of the category to record it. Often they will record into a miscellaneous file. When you have not seen it in a while, you may forget what the expense was. It might later be tagged to you as a personal expense, which could lead to you personally being responsible for it.

7. Keep all receipts. File them or scan them for easy reference when needed.

8. Track your expenses to be sure you are maintaining your budget.

9. Take the time to schedule regular meetings with the accountant to go over your finances face to face and on conference calls.

10. Tax evasion is illegal. Tax avoidance, however, is legal when utilizing the system in place to maximize deductions and credits.

11. Be sure to file your taxes on time.

12. Pay attention to the bottom line. Just because you are bringing in money every day does not mean you are making money. You could actually be losing money if you are paying out more than you are bringing in. Evaluate your expenses and income monthly so you can see the bottom line.

13. Know your monthly break-even point, the cost of doing business, and how much you will need to earn before producing your first dollar in profit.

14. Hire professionals who stay updated on the latest tax laws and regulations.

15. When you are just starting out, you may have to maintain your own records to keep expenses down, but you should still obtain an accountant's advice in setting up your recordkeeping system. This way, as you grow, turning the operations over to an accounting firm or bookkeeper will be smooth and less costly.

Take a tip from the many celebrities who have reported theft or mismanagement of their money. Don't let anyone take advantage of you.

Pay attention to your business finances!

YOUR BANKING NEEDS

Choose a bank carefully. You must know how your business is doing at all times. When you want to apply for a business loan, bond, or any other documents you may need, you will need to know that the paperwork that is provided to the bank is prepared accurately.

Build a Relationship With Your Bank Staff

When you go to the bank for assistance, you will want to know the people who make the decisions. Most of the time people just run in any branch and make their deposit or withdrawal as quickly as possible. Because of our busy lifestyles, we don't even know the teller who counts out the money.

Take the time to talk with the manager of your bank, get on a first-name basis, and let them become familiar with you and your business. Then when you have a concern, you can pick up the phone, ask for that particular person by name, and speak with someone who knows your name and your business.

Pay attention. Get to know the names of the tellers and loan officers you meet in your visits to the bank and establish a friendly relationship.

Select Advice That Works for You

When I was looking to get someone to finance my mortgage, my credit was shot. Usually the banks will not secure a loan when the credit profile is weak. But I spoke with the manager who knew me and was aware of my circumstances and he went out of his way to assist me.

He explained the underwriting process, and advised me on the best approach. He went on to tell me that because my credit score was so low, I would need to produce a hardship letter. He gave me advice about what to say and how to say it.

Although I was grateful for his help, some of his advice wasn't right for me. He wanted me to apologize and state that I had made poor decisions that had resulted in our financial difficulties. However, I knew I had done what was best for me at the time. I hadn't paid all of my bills on time. If I had, I would not have had the money to create my own business. I really needed to take everything we had and put it into our dream. All of my faith, my commitment, and my drive were necessary to make it work.

I knew I would do better if given the opportunity. And looking back, I wouldn't change a thing.

I had an unwavering belief that when it did work out, I would not only be in position to change our state of affairs, but I would be able to help countless others.

I wrote the hardship letter differently than the banker had advised. In my letter, I told them exactly what I did. I explained that in order for me to succeed, I had to stop paying everybody and remain focused on the end result. I explained that within three years, I had totally turned our business around, as well as our lives. I paid all of my creditors in full — no settlements — and at this point I owed nothing. If I had to do it again, I wouldn't change a thing. My banker submitted the letter, and spoke with the underwriters on my behalf. They gave me the loan.

If you are turned down by a bank, it does not mean you cannot get the loan, it only means you must become creative. You can reapply with new information. There is more than one bank to serve you and there are different bankers and loan officers to speak with you. Go back to the drawing board, refocus, and think about what information or resources you did not explore. How can you repackage the information?

Stay focused on your goal using your head, not your heart. Obstacles are only illusions that will either melt you down, or build you up. It is the challenges you face that will build the character and discipline you need to be in business.

In all of your undertakings, cultivate professional relationships. You never know whose assistance you may need when establishing your own business. These relationships can be for a reason, a season, or a lifetime.

A friendship founded on business is better than a business founded on friendship.

~John D. Rockefeller

Lessons Learned: Seek Professional Advice, But Follow Your Beliefs

- Create personal relationships with your bank's personnel and ask for advice when you need it.

- Don't compromise your beliefs. Your beliefs make you who you are. While I am not advising you to be inflexible, you don't want to feel as if you are actually working toward something that is in opposition to your beliefs.

- Don't become emotionally defeated by the challenge in front of you.

Chapter Nine

Mentors and Mentoring

A MENTOR CAN MAKE ALL THE DIFFERENCE

When I worked for other people in a company, I always felt like the little guy. I could never see myself in a higher position because I always thought I was not good enough; not smart enough. I certainly never felt that I could be the Chief Executive Officer (CEO).

The job dictated my life and everything I did. I was told what to do, when to do it, how it should be done, when to eat, when to be finished eating, when to go home, when to spend time with my family, when I could take a vacation, how much time I would be allowed, how much I could spend, what stores I could shop in, what kind of car I could drive, and which neighborhoods I could afford. I had bought into a lifestyle that didn't fit me.

Mrs. James triggered an awakening in my soul. Her mentorship was our greatest asset. We pursued our dream with her support and I did become CEO of my own company.

Mrs. James, as you have already read, started us on our journey. Along the way, she was our constant inspiration. We asked her advice at every opportunity, and later, we followed her example by assisting other beginning entrepreneurs when our business became a success.

Having a mentor made all the difference to us in our personal growth as well as in the growth of our business.

Because of Mrs. James' mentoring, Preston and I were able to help many people. We were blessed to be able to contribute in many ways.

My perspective completely changed. When working in a job for someone else, I could not see past my own backyard. Working for myself, I had a new opportunity to make a difference in the lives of others, and I took it every chance I got.

If you are lucky, you already have met some people who may be willing to mentor you. This person will hold such an important position in your life and career. You must choose wisely. Each mentor has different beliefs and philosophies. Make sure you acquire one who has obtained success in your industry.

What kind of person makes a good mentor?

What qualities should you look for?

CHARACTERISTICS OF A GOOD MENTOR

- A business mentor may be a retired colleague, an industry leader, a professor, or an entrepreneur. Mrs. James was a retired leader in my industry.

- A mentor has the desire to share their experience and knowledge so they can make a difference in the lives of others as they begin their career. Mrs. James said she had done everything she had wanted to do and at this point in her life she could only see more success through the eyes of others she helped. This is the kind of attitude a good mentor should have.

- A mentor is someone who has developed credibility over time, faced adversity and challenge, and has grown successfully from it. They have earned a good reputation and the respect of their peers. I saw this clearly in the way others industry leaders respected Mrs. James. They listened to her advice and respected her approach to the concerns and issues they faced in business.

- Your mentor can see opportunities for you even when you don't see them. Mrs. James suggested that we open the school, and more important, she believed that we could do it. She helped us see her vision and believe in it.

- Mentors have contacts and relationships that can open doors for you in ways that you may not foresee. Mrs. James introduced me to influential leaders who helped me to obtain contracts.

- A mentor can be someone you call on for one-on-one help. They can be valuable teachers. I will never forget the day I called Mrs. James in a panic at 4:30 in the morning because I had a lesson to teach that day and I was not familiar with the subject. She asked me to take out my book. She went through that chapter with me with a fine-toothed comb and gave me all kinds of anecdotes and stories to bring the lesson home. She helped me gain a thorough understanding of the topic. And when I taught it, I nailed it.

- Your mentor stimulates your growth by forcing you to think outside of the box, changing your mind and your behavior so you can reach your desired results. When I didn't have the furniture to meet the requirements to open the school, she made me think about the requirements from a new perspective. The regulations did not say *new* furniture. She helped me to think outside of the box to meet all of the requirements. We did it and stayed on course, meeting our deadline to open.

- A mentor will shorten your learning curve and can help you streamline the process of beginning your business. You will have hands-on experience and one-on-one interaction that is focused mainly on you and your goals. Although many people have started a business at the same time we did, many of the ones practicing traditional methods of business taught in schools have since closed. We were able to have interaction with Mrs. James regularly and this accelerated our growth to success. We were able to avoid many of the pitfalls that others fall victim to in the first five years of being in business.

- Your mentor reinforces your belief in your business when you are knocked down, and helps keep you focused on your goals. Many times I was challenged with naysayers and those who felt we didn't know what we were doing. I sometimes took this personally because somewhere in my brain I feared that what they were saying was true. But to Mrs. James, none of it made sense in her mind.

Her response was always something like:

Don't give in to negativity. Stay Focused. Everything is in Divine Order.

When I didn't know how to respond to negativity she would remind me:

It's not what happens to you, it's what happens in you. You must stay focused and you will put all of this behind you. It will get better.

- A mentor will forbid excuses. Don't make excuses for not taking on a task. Find a way to do it. As they say, you can't make excuses and money at the same time.

- Your mentor cares about your long-term development. Mrs. James talked with me about the future growth of my business and made recommendations to me for investments that would sustain my lifestyle long after I retire from the business. We spoke daily and she stayed in Michigan for five years until she felt that I was ready to move on independently; only then she moved to Texas.

APPROACH SUCCESSFUL PEOPLE

How do you find a mentor?

For us, it was a matter of recognizing and accepting Mrs. James as a mentor when she appeared in front of us. We were lucky; Mrs. James came to us right at the beginning of our journey. We had just adopted our entrepreneurial mindset and were searching for a building to start our business. If you are ready to proceed, you may find, like we did, that help will appear — you just need to recognize it.

Even when we had just met her, we knew something about her was different. *I believed her.* I believed that if she believed in us, that we could do it. I didn't know the woman but she seemed genuine to me. I hung on her every word.

We were lucky that we recognized the value of Mrs. James as a mentor early in our career. She taught us business-success principles, and opened our eyes to new horizons and the birth of our vision began. She helped us to think of ourselves differently — to create new beliefs about who we were and what we were capable of.

To find a mentor, you will need to be open to possibility, ready to recognize the right person, and willing to approach people in your field.

How to Approach Experts for Advice or Mentoring

First, find someone who is successfully doing what it is that you want to do. Ask them if you can take them out for coffee or lunch. If they are not available to have lunch with you, ask if they would take a ten-minute call with you at their convenience.

Let them know you admire them for their accomplishments and you would be ecstatic if they would oblige you by allowing a moment of their time to help you with a few decisions you need to make. Tell them you are interested in their perspective on how to increase your chances of success in your business. You will be surprised at the number of people willing to take time to speak with you, especially when you approach them with humility and sincerity.

Be ready to bring something to the table; always ask if there is anything you can do to assist them in return. Offer your services and be willing to provide it without asking for a wage, if you can manage it. When you work with someone who is already successful in your field, it will be an immensely valuable learning experience for you. Any kind of hands-on training in your business will enhance your capacity to think, create, and grow.

Business Workshops

During my business growth, I contacted Dan Gilbert, the owner of Quicken Loans (formerly Rock Financial), by sending an email message to him asking for advice. His secretary called me back for a conference call with him on the line. He not only took the time to listen to me and advise me, but he also invited me to attend one of the workshops that he personally facilitates for his management team. This was a priceless opportunity that allowed me to learn how major multi-million-dollar companies prioritize tasks and build their businesses.

As our business began to thrive, Preston and I took time to go to North Carolina to meet industry leaders Joe and Eunice Dudley, owners of Dudley Products and Beauty Schools. I had admired this company and their business operation for years and I just wanted to meet them, talk with them, and learn from them.

What an amazing experience it was. Mr. Dudley personally took Preston and me, in his car, to his corporate office. He introduced us to their staff. They loved working for the Dudley's and it showed in everything they did. We toured the plant where his products were made.

We had dinner together at his school cafeteria and he took us to his home. The Dudley's sat down with us and gave us some very important advice about business. I especially enjoyed talking about excerpts of Napoleon Hill's *Think and Grow Rich* with them. Mr. Dudley shared with us how he was able to grow his business and gave us some pointers. He allowed me to speak with his teams during his morning meetings.

The visit was a valuable experience that will always be with us; we would reflect on the Dudley's advice many times over the next several years.

Building Relationships With Others in the Industry

Over the years I have found that building relationships is a vital part of building strength in your business. Close professional relationships will help you with your business networking, and can assist with information gathering and problem-solving.

When speaking with other beauty school owners early in my career, I realized that we were all concerned with similar issues: student recruitment, education, staff management, and the common operations of our kind of business. At times, being able to share our ideas helped immensely with decision-making processes.

Once I ran a radio advertisement to bring new students into my school. As a result I obtained many students. I was later contacted by two other school owners for my assistance. They wanted to know how I was attracting so many students and if I could help them. For some reason, they had tried, applied themselves, and hadn't had any success. Their schools had few students while my school was flourishing.

One of the owners I knew personally; she had a school located less than two miles from me. The other school owner I did not know.

Others warned me that assisting these owners could be a bad strategy for my business.

I heard comments like:

- "You cannot help them; they are your rivals."

- "Who helps their competition like that?"

- "They will take all of your clients."

Whenever I heard comments like these, I tried to explain that there is enough room in this world for everyone. I wanted to help others if I could. After all, if ever the shoe were on the other foot, I would want someone to reach out to me.

I gave these two school owners specific information and guided them through the process. They ran profitable schools. We all remained friends and years later, when both school owners closed their facility and I needed teachers, both of them came to work for me and were exceptional leaders.

Lessons Learned: Mentoring

- Keep your eyes open for good mentors; sometimes they are right in front of you and you just need to recognize them.

- Seek expert advice, especially if you are new to an industry.

- Help others in the field when you become a success.

- Do not hesitate to help mentor a competitor. Do not be afraid that someone can take your dream away. They will never see your vision through their eyes, and neither will you be able to see theirs. Wish them well in all of their endeavors.

Chapter Ten

Client Relationships

CLIENT RELATIONSHIPS

My best friend Kellee, a real estate agent, was speaking with a lady she just met at a conference. They talked about their children, their parents, their travels, and fell out laughing about the good ole days. She said they hit it off as though they had known each other for years and they exchanged numbers.

The lady called Kellee the next day and told her she was given a referral to contact a real estate agent, but she would feel so much more comfortable if Kellee would assist her in her purchase instead. Kellee hadn't spoken much about real estate in their conversation, but she had established a rapport. The lady wanted to be around Kellee because she felt comfortable with her. People don't buy the business, they buy you.

You are mistaken if you feel that clients frequent your business solely because of your knowledge and your skills. You are in the people business. When they don't like *you*, they don't buy from you.

Often, people don't know what they want when they arrive. They rely on you, because you are an expert and a professional, to make them comfortable from the start. From the time they walk in the door until the time they leave, they are deciding whether they will return. Leave an impression about you that your clients will remember, one that will bring them back to you and will encourage them to share their experience with friends.

Here are some question for you to think about:

- What do you do to give your clients a positive experience?

- How is your customer service better or different than the competition?

- How is the environment? Is it fresh and appealing?

- Do you offer extras that the client does not expect?

- Do you *wow* your customers on occasions with something new or something different?

- How do they feel about the entire experience after the service is done?

BUILDING TRUST AND A GOOD REPUTATION

Clients come to you because they have a problem that they want solved and they trust that you have answers. They need your expertise. If they could do it themselves, they wouldn't need you. In addition, they have chosen you over many other providers who are available.

- Never take your clients for granted. With technology today, recognize that your customer has the opportunity to surf and choose from a wide variety of businesses. Although you may have cutting-edge service, they can always find similar services online.

- Take their trust seriously. Always give your best quality service.

- Keep your certifications current.

- Update your techniques consistently so you can solve their problems efficiently.

- The key to success in any business is to maintain exemplary customer service. Your customers want to know that you care about their needs. Create a *Customer First* approach as part of your business system.

- Survey your clientele continuously to find out what they are thinking about your business. Review the surveys regularly and implement change as needed. Don't ignore this step. It is crucial to the future of your business.

Stand By Your Service or Product

Desiree was having a perm done on her hair when she experienced bad burns to her scalp after the product was left on too long. Although the operator tried all she could to relieve her of the pain, Desiree later experienced some hair falling out as a result of the burns. She had scabs on her scalp. Because she traveled a good distance to go to the salon, she didn't want to go back the next day to complain about it to the stylist or the owners. She had been happy with her prior experiences at the salon and had liked the way they styled her hair.

She called the salon to let them know the condition of her hair and scalp. They apologized and wanted her to come back immediately, but when she explained that it was too far to travel, they told her they would treat her condition whenever she could come, and in addition, her next hair appointment would be complimentary.

Desiree now speaks of this as a positive experience to others and expresses her appreciation for good customer service. She has a commitment to be loyal to those who are loyal to her and continues to be a customer at the same salon.

Failures are a part of business. You don't win them all. But how you handle mistakes will make a huge difference in the long run. People buy from those who stand behind their product. Be willing to fix any mistakes immediately; don't ignore a situation for the sake of convenience. Go out of your way to please your clients.

Customer service skills must be practiced and mastered so that you can avoid embarrassing situations that could cause you to lose customers or miss opportunities to gain new clients.

Think about Desiree. What if, instead of calling the salon, she had just decided not to come back?

With no positive resolution to her problem, she probably would have gone on to share her bad experience with others. Salons depend on local business, so imagine the result if Desiree had told ten friends *not* to get their hair done at that salon. Over the course of a year, the salon would have lost Desiree's business and potentially, the business of ten other people. Instead, Desiree continued to be a customer and it is likely that, feeling happy about the resolution of her problem, she would recommend the salon to other women.

Here is another important question: What made Desiree call instead of just resolving never to return?

This is much more likely to happen when a customer feels a personal connection with the owner or operator of a business.

Do Your Clients Return?

How are your people skills? Reputation and repeat business will tell you a great deal about the quality of your customer service.

Do your clients return? Clients are smart and they know what they want. If they sense you don't care, they won't be back.

If customers aren't coming back, choose to fix it by improving your personal skills. If you truly care about people and you love what you do, you won't have to boast about yourself, they will do it for you. If they are not doing just that, then you know you need to make improvements.

How important is it to keep your customers coming back? According to White House Office of Consumer Affairs, it is six to seven times more costly to attract a new customer than it is to retain an existing customer.

As the owner of the business, you are the star of the show. You must make your clients love you. Get to know them by name and develop a pleasing relationship with them. This is your business; your reputation is always at stake.

When the clients leave your door, they will speak about their experience with others. Years down the road they may forget the components of your product, the names of your employees, or the details of the transaction, but they will remember how they were treated and they will remember meeting the owner. The impression you leave with them will stand out, for better or worse, so make sure it is a conversation that you would be proud of. Make the extra effort to give each client your personal attention.

You can spend money on advertising and work relentlessly to build your business, but you must work just as hard to make your clients feel that they are appreciated. Think of customer service as the front line of your business. Of course, some clients are finicky and you cannot please everyone all the time, but you should always try to make every client feel respected.

TALKING TO POTENTIAL CLIENTS

I listened outside the door of the office once while my new enrollment officer was consulting with a prospect about the benefits of attending our school. The prospect was referred to our school by a graduate and she was inquiring about the possibility of attending at a future date.

The enrollment officer spoke about the start dates, ending dates, history, the training, the wonderful teachers, the advanced training, the awesome training kits, the testimonials of graduates and employers, hair shows and trade shows, and she told them about the travel opportunities to national and international shows. Her speech was filled to the brim with information.

I peeked into the office and interrupted the enrollment officer, asking if she could be excused for a moment so I could speak with her. In private, I told her about the importance of finding out what a prospect wanted first, before following up by building up the value of our solution to her problem. I asked her to sit in for a moment while I spoke with the prospect.

Sitting with the prospect, the first thing I asked her was why she was inquiring about our program. I let her talk. I then asked her what she liked about this career, and if she had special talent or experience. I asked her if she knew anyone in the field. Each time I asked her a question, I just let her talk about herself and I listened.

I asked her if this was a career that she would want to someday open as her own business and she said yes.

She had a child with her and I asked her child's name. I asked her if the business idea was a legacy that she would like to leave for her children. She said yes. I asked her if she had a lot of time to spend with the children. She said no. We talked about the benefits of working part-time so we could spend more time at home with children. I asked her to tell me how she thought this career might benefit her family.

I asked her how much money she would like to earn and if she felt this career could bring her that kind of success. She said yes. I asked her how she thought this might happen and I just listened while she talked about her vision of the future.

Finally, I asked her how long she thought it might be before she cashed her first paycheck as a stylist.

She said, "I'm ready *now!*"

I told her she could come back the next day to bring in her deposit. She returned with her deposit the same day and started the program.

The Personal Touch

A personal touch is powerful in client relations. When you are talking to clients, give them your full person-to-person attention. Think of your product or service as a way to help a client with their personal lives in some way.

Although you may have a beautiful location, great testimonies, and good-hearted staff members, your prospective clients will be focused on their own lives, and how to solve their own personal problems.

While talking to you, they may be thinking:

- How will this make a difference in my life?

- How can this help my children get through this hard time?

- How can I help my ailing parents?

- Will I be able to make my car payments?

- How will my children ever afford to go to college?

- How can I stop this pain?

- Will I ever be able to get an apartment so I can get out of my parents' house?

- I'm so tired; how can I do it all?

- Can I really open my own business?

- What if I'm not smart enough or skilled enough to do what I need to do?

- How can I be more energetic, more successful, healthier and more confident?

Your clients are not concerned as much with your list of accomplishments and services as they are concerned with their own lives and problems. If you can solve one or more of their problems, you will have a client for life.

As you can see from the prospective client interview example in the last section, when people are going through turmoil in their lives, they tend to forget their dreams and you can help them to remember.

Asking questions and allowing the client to talk about themselves is always a good conversational tactic in these cases.

In the course of talking about themselves, they will remember what they want and why they came to you. They will end up telling you why they need your service; you will just answer their questions and give them information they might find useful.

Let them become captivated by their own dreams and desires as they talk to you. Ideally, you won't have to sell them on the benefits of your service. They will tell what they want, and will appreciate you for listening.

When it is clear what they want, you can open their minds to the opportunities in front of them—the ones that can help them to make a difference in their lives. Create the vision to show them what it looks like if they buy. Ask them thought-provoking questions that will stir their imagination. Let them know that their problem can be solved with your solution.

Be focused on personal elements so it is clear to your clients that you are paying attention to their needs. Remember their names and take notes so you can recall later what their needs and concerns are.

This personal touch goes a long way toward establishing long-term customers.

My son-in-law Rick goes out of his way to get coffee every morning from the same coffee shop. When he goes through the drive-through and orders a small coffee with half cream and half sugar, he hears through the speaker, "Coming right up, Rick!"

This business owner has made it a policy for staff members to remember their regular clients' names and their special orders. Even though his wife makes a great cup of coffee at home, this courtesy is the reason Rick goes out of his way to return each day.

Build in the Details

One day I was running late taking my four grandkids to the movies.

I was rushing to get the tickets when Kai, the four-year-old said, "Grandma, we have to get the popcorn."

I explained that we would miss the movie if I stopped for popcorn because the movie had already started. Since they had just eaten dinner, my plan was to get the popcorn after the movie was over. I quickly pushed them into the theater and we sat down.

After only five minutes, Kai, who sat next to me, said, "Grandma, can you go get the popcorn now?"

I explained to her in a whisper that I was the only adult here and couldn't leave them all by themselves. We would get popcorn later. The entire time, I could see her through my peripheral vision staring at me every few seconds with disgust for not getting the popcorn. I don't think she enjoyed the movie at all.

As soon as the movie was over I told her we could go get the popcorn on the way out.

Kai looked at me, still disappointed, and said, "It's too late Grandma. We are supposed to eat the popcorn while we watch the movie."

When I dropped her off, she yelled to her mother, "Grandma didn't buy us any popcorn."

That was the last impression she had about that trip with Grandma. I never forgot the popcorn again.

What is the lesson here? How does this apply to your business?

Lessons Learned: Building in the Details

Don't leave out the details when you are planning an experience for customers. Prepare ahead of time, anticipate the outcome and give a lasting impression. Leaving out the popcorn was a disappointment to Kai because she trusted that this would make the movie time enjoyable. It was a major part of Kai's experience, not just the movie. What a lesson I learned!

For your customers, you must include those little things that make people feel good to be in your care, and maintain this kind of attention to detail over time.

Have you ever gone into a business that totally wowed you initially, but with time, the quality of your experience diminished?

Think about Disney World. How would people feel if they neglected to perform the 3:00 parade? Or if they only set off the fireworks on some days and not others? These events are prepared far in advance and occur every single day. All around the world, people trust that they will have the experience they expect when they go to Disney World. The customer experience is all about the details. Leave some of them out and the customer will be disappointed.

Your business must follow the same path. When you create a wow effect, small or large, they will remember the experience and expect it or something greater the next time they return to your business. Never give them less. When you diminish the experience, you leave an open window for your client to seek other businesses.

Imagine if you went to Disney and found Mickey Mouse missing? When you become a client and enjoy a certain kind of experience and later find that experience diminished, you will feel disappointed and disenchanted. It is worth the time and energy to give your clients a positive experience.

Before a play or concert opens, you know that it has taken months to prepare and set up. Somebody has figured out the choreography and script, the lighting, the music, the setting, and theme, the costumes and props. The staff have put a great deal of thought into design, promotion, and marketing, and all of this is for you, the customer, in the hope that you will be glued to your seat. Think about the last event you went to. How did you feel when you left? Did you feel that someone really prepared the details for you? Were you wowed? Or were you disappointed?

My bank served freshly baked macadamia cookies to clients each day when handling their banking transactions. It probably cost a hundred dollars a week to maintain the supply. Some people would stop in to make a transaction just to get a couple of cookies, including me! I didn't want to leave that bank because of the customer service; all of those small details gave me a positive experience that I wouldn't want to give up.

This applies to everyday business on a daily basis. Consider the role of the hotdog at a baseball game, the candied apples at a cider mill, and the holiday scents at a department store in the fall. All of these little details are part of the customer experience and they create a lasting impression.

The Harley-Davidson company has used this kind of approach expertly for over a hundred years. They never focus on just selling a product; they sell an experience.

In the case of my granddaughter, Kai, what she enjoyed about watching a movie wasn't just the movie; it was the overall experience of being out in a theater immersed in the environment. This included the popcorn—the smell and the taste and the thrill of eating it in the theater while watching the movie with her grandmother. The movie itself wasn't the experience for her — the critical elements were in the associated details.

Don't forget to build in the details!

Treat Every Client With Respect

One day, my friend Brandy and I walked into a car dealership to find a conversion van for Preston's surprise birthday gift. We were dressed in jeans, gym shoes, and t-shirts. No salesperson came to greet us. We walked around by ourselves.

As we were looking at all of the luxury vans on the showroom floor, we spotted the one. It was white with a white leather interior. It was the best-looking van on the showroom floor. We looked around for help. We walked toward the office and spotted the car salesmen in their offices looking out the window.

Disappointed with the service, Brandy yelled, "Excuse me! Can we get some help?!"

At that moment, one man stepped forward. He said he was sorry; he thought the other guy was working with us. I told him I wanted the floor model and he went on to tell us about the vans outside on the lot that were more reasonable than the one I was looking at.

He obviously figured we could not afford it because of the way we were dressed. He was *wrong*. For me, the money was not an issue. We actually bought the van that day, in cash. He could have easily lost the sale because he prejudged us.

This reminds me of a similar story I read about the pianist, Herbie Hancock, who was in his early twenties back in 1963. His roommate, trumpeter Donald Byrd, told him about the new

Cobra that was faster than the Ferrari. Although Herbie was not interested in purchasing one at the time, he was intrigued by the conversation and wanted to see what this car looked like.

While in New York, he decided to visit a dealership showroom to take a peek at this car that Donald had told him about. Dressed in only jeans and a t-shirt, the car salesman assumed he was not a serious customer and did not give him the attention or respect he would have given a well-dressed man.

Herbie asked the car salesman if he could see the Cobra.

The salesman shunned him, telling him, "You can't afford that car."

It cost six thousand dollars, which was a large amount of money at the time. Angry to be misjudged in that way, Herbie told the man he would be back tomorrow to purchase that very car.

He came back and bought the car that he never intended to buy. What Herbie did not know at the time was that he was purchasing a very limited double-carburetor edition of the car. Only a thousand Cobras were produced and less than one hundred of those had a double carburetor.

He now owns the only double carburetor in existence that is still in original condition, making the value of his car currently over two million dollars. He is thankful for the salesman's rude behavior, because it inspired him to buy the car in the first place!

You never know who your next client will be. Treat every client with respect even if it appears doubtful that they can afford your services.

Express Your Joy

The way that you feel about your business will show when you are interacting with staff and clients. Don't forget; you are doing what you love to do. Let it show. Every day, express your joy for your work.

Help your employees to be happy as well. If you are enthusiastic about your business, it will be contagious.

APPEARANCE DOES MATTER

Have you ever wondered how much your appearance matters to the people you meet, or how much it matters in business?

Imagine for a moment that you are in a restaurant and you see a waiter, who has on a crisp, clean uniform, hair neatly combed, speaking with the clients at the table in front of you. He looks over at you with a smile, then quietly motions to you that he will be at your table next. How do you feel about the restaurant?

Now imagine that a different waiter comes to your table with a worn and dingy apron that looks as though it had drips of spaghetti sauce on it. His hair is unkempt.

He has a pad and pulls a pen from behind his ear and says impatiently, "Ready to order?"

Now how do you feel about the restaurant?

Although you may give him your order, the visual image and your perception of this person could change your mind about the establishment and the service.

For many people, appearance and presentation is very important and they spend a great deal of time working on their personal appearance. Both men and women are highly conscious of others' perceptions.

Economic studies show that we equate personal grooming with the level of income you make. In addition, we tend to expect professionals to take care with their appearance, and will more quickly put our trust in a person who looks well-groomed.

I often hear people say that they want to be comfortable in what they wear and wonder why they should have to wear a suit or uniform to work. The truth is that your appearance represents the business you are in.

If you are an accountant, lawyer, business professional or if you work in an office, most people would expect you to wear professional attire. People need to feel confidence in the people who serve them. Wearing professional attire inspires confidence; it says that you are capable of handling your business. On the other hand, if you work in specific trades or in IT computing it may be acceptable to dress in more casual attire.

Dressing to fit your business profile speaks volumes about your professionalism. Your image is always on stage. You are a direct representation of your vision and your company and so are the people who work with you.

You've heard it said that you never get a second chance to make a first impression. The fact is that when you first meet a client, he makes a judgment about you in approximately four seconds. Before you open your mouth, their brain is trying to make sense of whether they should hire you or not. You may win them over when you speak, but people believe what they see and feel first. A good portion of their judgment occurs in those first moments.

In fact, in a survey of American Personnel Consultants, who are men and women responsible for hiring people in large companies, it was found that most made their decision to hire or not within *thirty seconds* of the first meeting.

Everything that contributes to the way you look on the outside is important. If it's not helping you, it's hurting you.

You have total control over your dress and grooming. In fact, we generally assume that a person consciously and deliberately makes a personal statement about himself with every part of his appearance.

Clothes are responsible for 95 percent of the first impression that you make. Your makeup, your hairstyle, and other elements that determine your appearance from the neck up also influence the way that you are perceived. Your accessories, such as purse, briefcase, watch, tie, and jewelry, also make a statement.

If you are in sales or business, the way you are perceived by someone will largely determine the influence you have over him or her, and will strongly affect your level of credibility. In the area of personal credibility, everything counts.

Making a great first impression is imperative if you want to become an influential leader.

Remember when Mrs. James asked me to wear a blue suit for my first meeting? I didn't have a blue suit because I never had to attend a formal business meeting.

Everything in my closet was casual. I didn't have the money to purchase one at the time. So I went to a Salvation Army thrift store and found one in my size. When we arrived at the meeting, I cannot tell you the confidence I felt walking into that meeting with Mrs. James. When she introduced me to the other professionals as a new business owner whom she was mentoring, I felt like I belonged there. The women at the meeting felt comfortable speaking with me on business topics and I felt comfortable responding to them. I felt like I was already successful because I had dressed for the part.

When you dress to play the role, you set the tone and the stage of authority.

Here are some tips:

- Take complete control over every detail of your personal appearance and grooming; Resolve to look like a powerful, influential person in all your business activities.

- Study fashion and proper dress so you know exactly what to wear and in what combination.

- Understand what kind of dress is appropriate for your industry. Appearance varies depending on the profession, but you must always lead in your appearance.

- Make sure your clothes fit and compliment your figure, but don't be too sexy. Rich colors portray authority.

- Hair and nails should be neat and makeup understated.

- Wear comfortable, well-kept shoes. Avoid flip flops, sneakers or sporty sandals.

- Don't over-accessorize; don't wear distracting jewelry.

- Avoid strong perfumes.

In business, everyone follows your lead, so lead by example. Set the stage with the image you want to portray and make it mandatory that your staff conforms to your policy of appearance.

Chapter Eleven

Taking the Lead

CREATING POLICIES

Create a *Policy and Procedures Manual*. Before the game starts, you will want to make sure that the rules are clear so there are no misunderstandings. Enforcing policies may be new to you and it may feel awkward in the beginning, but you will come to understand that employees on a team want to know what the rules are and where the boundaries are. People want to do a great job by nature. Creating clear policy allows them the freedom to work according to the plan and within the guidelines.

A *Policy and Procedures Manual* will ensure that every step is followed through with efficiency. Think carefully about the contents of your manual:

- Outline every detail of your expectations for your employees.

- Give it to them on their first day and go over it with them periodically for clarity; they should sign off that they understand your policies.

- The manual should include the procedure for submitting a complaint. Be sure to follow up promptly on any complaints.

- It should be clear, in writing, that if they choose not to follow your policy and cause disruption to your business operation, they will be subject to disciplinary action as stated in your written policy.

- Always enforce your policies consistently, and follow them yourself.

It's good to be nice, but always be firm. Your employees are always watching your reaction in difficult circumstances. This allows them to know first-hand what you are made of and if you are the leader they want to follow. If you are disrespected or challenged and do nothing in response, it will affect your entire team and you will likely see more negative behavior as a result.

If this happens, you may have to clean house and start over. So get it right from the beginning. It is very difficult to regain respect and authority once you have lost it.

There are times when you will need to set an example even when it feels painful to you. When you do, you will not only gain the respect of your team, but you will reward the antagonist with a lesson that they will need to learn to move forward in their career.

It's very important that you lead by example and follow your own policies; stick with them and don't deviate. Applying structure to yourself is difficult to do as a new business owner. Many will set guidelines, but not adhere to their own policies when pushed.

"Do as I say, not as I do," is never a good policy for your business.

Be flexible, but only when necessary.

INTERVIEWING AND HIRING

Having the wrong person in the wrong position could cripple your growth.

What should you look for in an interview?

- Look for confidence. Successful people are self-reliant and confident in their abilities. No one develops into a recognized figure without great self-esteem. These people constantly outperform those who are unsure of themselves and their potential.

- Look for aspirations. Does your candidate aspire to be the best at what he does? Does she constantly challenge herself to be better?

- Look for ability. Does the candidate possess the talent you are looking for? Is there anything that would prevent this candidate from performing tasks? In your interview, use your questions to probe the candidate's ability to perform. In some cases you might want to develop a set of tasks for a candidate to perform so you can directly assess their capabilities.

- Look for willingness to work within *your* system. Remember, first impressions are signals of what you can expect. Can this candidate take constructive criticism? Are they open and willing to learn to do the job to your specifications?

- What about education and experience? In our early years, we tended to hire employees who possessed a master's degree and years of experience. They demanded a high rate of pay, but we thought that their education and years of experience would add value to our program. We later found that this was not necessarily so. We found that although they had the experience, some of them had learned a lot of shortcuts along the way and had lost sight of the core values that were necessary to perform the job at peak perfection. Using these shortcuts for so long, they themselves forgot how to perform the basic tasks, so they actually brought little value to my system.

Orientation

Give your new employees solid ground so they can hit the ground running by preparing an *Orientation Day* prior to the first day of work. This sets the tone for the business culture and expectations. An orientation gives them an opportunity to ask questions, go over your business rules and regulations—and agree to comply—and decide if they can embrace your business from the start.

Be sure to plan the day out with care. You might include some role playing to demonstrate proper customer service, create some videos, and engage them in other forms of creative training designed to help them understand what is expected of them.

In addition:

- Go over policies and procedures.

- Create a test from your *Policies and Procedures Manual* and give it to them to be sure that they understand your business and the culture. Have them sign it.

- Give everyone a detailed *Job Description*.

- Carefully craft an *Employment Agreement* that caters to your particular business and have new employees review and sign it.

- Have everyone sign a *Non-Disruption Agreement* that says that they understand that they will not spread ugly gossip throughout your business, or cause negative confrontations with the staff.

Training

Hire quality employees, train them well, and monitor their progress. Follow through regularly to be sure that you and your staff are on a path that is in alignment with your mission and vision.

We developed our own training system to ensure success. Remember to always *inspect what you expect* and follow up regularly.

We developed surveys and distributed them regularly to customers. This allowed us to know if our employees were performing to customer expectations. Anonymous surveys from clients can be a wake-up call for employees. One of our employees cried while reviewing her surveys — she thought she had been doing a tremendous job, but her client surveys let her know that they thought she was slow getting started, seemed unprepared and distracted, and did not seem friendly or approachable.

She had no idea that this was what they thought of her. The biggest letdown to her was that they stated that they would not recommend her services to anyone. She was embarrassed and ashamed, but was also determined to improve. She knew she had to take ownership of her actions and she knew she could do better if she was willing to have an open mind to constructive criticism.

She began to work diligently on her performance, her attitude, and her skills. Her next performance review was tremendous!

She felt much better at the rave reviews and vowed to maintain this level of performance. Help your employees become awesome and they will stay there. When someone goes from mediocre to feeling awesome about their work, they will never want to go back to mediocre again!

MAKE THE MOST OF MEETINGS

Meetings are necessary for communication and decision-making, but if they are not well-managed, they can feel like a waste of time.

Do your meetings feel interminable?

Does the discussion often stray so you never get through the actual agenda?

Do you end meetings knowing you haven't accomplished anything of substance?

We had all of these problems at one time. Not surprisingly, people were not excited to attend these meetings. They were boring, long, and unproductive. Attendees would constantly look at their watches, and would literally run out of the door when the time was up.

They didn't learn anything new and nothing valuable was gained for attending the meeting. Nobody felt that we had made the best use of the time spent. We researched other ways to facilitate meetings and gradually began to improve the process.

Here are the strategies that we found to be the most helpful:

- When you are planning a meeting, try to create an experience that is valuable to everyone. Everybody's time should be treated as important.

- Carefully select the topics to discuss and stick to the agenda.

- For each topic, prepare in advance the direction you want to go and the kind of delivery necessary to give clear instruction for the discussion.

- Decide the maximum amount of time you will spend on each of the topics.

- Designate a time-keeper.

- Commit to stay focused and don't allow the meetings to stray onto tangent topics.

These strategies allowed our meetings to be short and to-the-point without unproductive chatter. They began to be a valuable use of time instead of a waste of time; there was no fat in our meetings. Accordingly, the attendees were much more engaged and, instead of running out the door, they often wanted to stay overtime to further a discussion.

REPRIMAND IN PRIVATE

Lakia and I were once invited by a client to join a meeting she had scheduled with her team. It was evident that she was angry about many things that were going wrong. In front of the entire team, she discussed what was done wrong and who was responsible. The tone of her voice exhibited anger and pain.

As she was talking, Lakia secretly slipped her a note that said: *Praise in public; reprimand in private.*

She glanced at the note, took a deep breath, and immediately changed her disposition and her tone. Her team began to relax, and to embrace the information.

She later said, "Lakia was absolutely right."

She told me that reading that note was like a slap in her face; the truth in it suddenly hit her like a ton of bricks.

When she changed the tone of the meeting, they discussed updates and information and the meeting was productive for all. She then thanked and praised everyone individually for their particular contribution to the company and privately she spoke with those that she had issues with.

If you have individuals who are not producing to your expectations, speak with them in private about ways to improve. This will help to alleviate negativity from the receiver and it will help them to see your point.

Never, ever, reprimand an employee in front of their peers. It is demeaning, disrespectful and creates an uncomfortable situation for everyone. If you have an audience listening while you are reprimanding someone, the person being reprimanded will focus their attention on who is listening and how embarrassing it is. There is no need to compound the problem with embarrassment and discomfort for everyone around.

However, under certain conditions, you may choose to have the person's manager in the room when you're talking, if you think it will foster communication. Also, at rare times it may be advisable to have a witness with you if you are discussing very serious or legal issues. No matter what the circumstances, you should always be steady, solid and professional. Preserve the dignity of your workplace.

If you ever find yourself angry at work, your employees should never see this. If you are angry with an employee, put off discussion. Ask them to leave, if necessary and make an appointment to speak at a later time. Your anger should be taken home to cool down and when you feel you have a level head, attend to the situation.

PRAISE IN PUBLIC

People will often work harder for recognition and a little praise than they would work for simply a paycheck. In every organization, these are the unsung heroes. This person works diligently behind the scenes and is usually invisible because they just get things done. You already know that you don't need to micro-manage them, or tell them what to do because they are always trying to do a good job. You always know that they have your back. Let them know how much you appreciate them. Take special time to get to know them personally.

Learn to praise people publicly and they will feel good about their accomplishments and want more. Praise results of your team's effort in front of everyone and they'll even start cheering each other on.

Catch individuals doing something right and do something nice for them by letting them know that you noticed. When you take care of your people, they will take care of you. Help your team see your vision for the future and their role in yours. Make them feel a part of something bigger than themselves and let them feel you care. Give them an opportunity to see that you are not just in business for you.

INSPIRE YOUR TEAM

- Take note of their birthdays and bring in a balloon or a cake with a card that you personally sign. Each person should have their own day.

- Give your employee of the month a gift card.

- Consider offering a day off for special occasions.

- Have a family night to get to know their children or family. Try hosting an event at an upcoming feature movie at the theater, a play, or other family gathering activities.

- Surprise the team with pizza day every now and then. Treat them to breakfast on a special day, especially a milestone or anniversary for your business. After all, they helped you get there.

- Send a particularly diligent team member out for specialized training and have them to come back and to present it to the rest of the team. Or hire a presenter to give training to the whole team.

- When someone does something nice for you, give a small gift of love, like a candy bar with a sweet note that says something about their kind gesture.

- Make a habit of writing post-it notes that say: "You did a great job. Thank you."

- Show up at some personal functions to show support, when invited.

- When they are sick, take them some soup or a soup cup with treats in it. When someone is troubled, offer them the day off and check on them.

People Follow Those They Respect

Whether you are a leader or an employee, speaking to others using profanity will diminish the respect people have for you, although they won't generally say anything.

Think to yourself: *Is this the vision I have for my company? Is this the image I want to portray to those who know me?*

I once saw an educator get angry with a student for speaking out in class. She yelled at the student, "Sit your a.... down!"

Shocked by the educator's demeanor and embarrassed by her tone, the student turned to her and yelled back angrily, using profanity, acting as if she was ready to fight.

This is a clear case of: *You get what you give.*

Her language caused an extreme negative reaction in the student, and the rest of the students were upset as well. They were surprised, and were angry with the educator; they expected the leader to handle the situation with more professionalism. They did not support her behavior.

The focus of the situation became the teacher's lost temper and the class lost respect for her because of it. Always remember to think before you speak. There are always consequences to your actions.

Think hard about the possible outcome the next time you are faced with a challenging situation that could cause you to lose it. Always focus on the good in people first; then, determine your next move. Be honest and diplomatic. Stay mindful of the way you treat others. Respect is a give and take proposition.

THE POWER OF DELEGATION

Have you ever started a project and become overwhelmed at the thought of everything in front of you that must be done by a deadline? This is the time to delegate.

If you want to get something done, leverage your time; find ways to use it most efficiently. Divide the job, then delegate tasks to people you know are responsible, reliable, and talented enough to get it done. Leaders know the power of delegation. You can get more done in less time and it will free up time that can be used to better oversee the project. But good delegation also requires follow up. Prior to the deadline you must be sure to inspect what you expect. Waiting until the last minute can be a disaster; give your team enough time to fix any mistakes, or small errors that may have resulted from poor communication.

Do you tend to work all day and all night to get the work done by yourself, because you don't trust others to do it as well as you?

It won't get done right if I don't do it.

Is this your mantra?

Get over it! The truth may be that you will always work harder than anyone else, but you also deserve a life.

I would rather earn 1 percent of one hundred people's efforts than 100 percent of my own.

~ John D. Rockefeller

People who know the value of delegation often show amazing results. Conversely, leaders who can't delegate are limited to what their own arms and legs can accomplish, and a business founded by such a person wouldn't go far.

If you struggle with this skill, be assured that delegation is learnable.

Create a team with the best talents to get the job done.

Learn to spend your valuable time organizing the team and structuring the plays on a map as a football coach does, rather than handling all of the small tasks yourself. You will become efficient in getting more things done quickly and effectively, in a fraction of the time.

Your time is valuable; learn to use it wisely.

You have projects that need to be handled and you have people who are capable of handling them, many of whom would embrace the opportunity to show you their strengths. When you effectively and clearly delegate, you will be surprised at how people will step up and get the job done.

Be clear about your expectations. Do not give a task to someone who has not shown the skill and confidence to work independently.

You can help members of your team to develop these abilities by guiding them through small projects at first, watching over them before giving them an independent task.

In our company we found it necessary to do a careful review of our operation regularly for a systematic approach to consistent processes and procedures. We created fourteen standards that the school utilized to measure the effectiveness of our programs.

This report is intensive and very important to our company, and we now delegate specific parts of it to team members, to review for accuracy and solicit documentation for verification. Each part must be submitted by a deadline so that we can review it at regular meetings to be sure we are meeting our goals and objectives.

At one time, this report was done solely by Lakia Hairston, the president of our company. The task was daunting when accomplished singlehandedly, so she decided to dissect the report and tap into the talented team of individuals around her. She delegated the entire report and she monitored and coached the team to a great outcome. As a result, she was able to use her own time more efficiently, which added more value to the company.

PLUCKING THE BAD APPLES

Whenever you are leading a team member who is not in compliance with the system, give them the opportunity to modify their behavior. Write down the limitation or behavior that needs change. Review it with the individual discussing your expectations and the opportunity to change, then have them sign and date it the same day.

If at all possible, have this completed right away. When you address the person, be clear that you are acting to monitor the effectiveness of everyone in balance with the system, not their behavior. You are in control of the success system. Behavior modification is not your job; it is theirs.

Don't be afraid that they will quit or that they will have an attitude with you. Everyone must comply with the system or it is not going to work. Remember, behavior modification is not your job; it is theirs.

If you have a bad apple in your business that you truly can't work with, get rid of them before they infect all of your good apples. But first, try speaking with the individual. Make him or her feel valued. Try to get the person to work with you in a productive way. Then, if they continue to be a negative force, let them go.

Keeping an incorrigible employee will only prolong your suffering and could possibly hurt the rest of the team. Never ever allow yourself to be ridiculed or disrespected by the people you lead. If you allow this with one, others will eventually follow.

Setting the tone and culture of your business is your responsibility. You are seeking to create harmony within your team, so at times you need to get rid of agitators who cause conflict. Let your team know that you are a no-nonsense business owner and you will not tolerate disrespect—toward you or your staff members. You must take a leadership role and remain consistent in your standards. You will gain respect from the team as they begin to see that they are following a strong leader.

Knowing When to Let Someone Go

I wore many hats in the early years. Some of my tasks:

- Opening up in the morning and closing at the end of the day
- Answering the phone and the door
- Enrolling students
- Assisting the instructors
- Attending to student needs
- Filing and record-keeping
- Writing letters and answering mail
- Purchasing supplies
- Collecting payments
- Shoveling snow and sweeping the sidewalk
- Cleaning the building in the evening

And when I got home, I still needed to do the cooking and cleaning. I had to take care of the kids, making sure they got their homework done, had their baths, and got ready for the next day. In those early days, I had hardly any time for my husband.

This was a tough time.

I was crazy busy all the time. I found it difficult to grow the business while I was still working in the business because I had too many hats to wear.

I was blessed to have a friend who volunteered to relieve me of some of the front desk work while I attended other duties. She wanted to help me and had great intentions but did not possess the friendly skills needed to bring in new business, nor did she have the outgoing personality that's needed to run the front desk. She was slow in signing up customers and responding to requests.

I knew she meant well. I appreciated her generosity. But then, the day came that she rudely treated a client on the phone.

She felt he was taking so long to get his point across, so she interrupted him and said in a very stern tone, "Can you hurry it up, because I have other people calling?"

Of course, it angered the client, so much so that he felt the need to come down to the school to confront her and to tell me about his experience. I was alarmed and embarrassed. I spoke with her about it and she swore that she would never to do that again.

But soon afterward, she overheard a client saying something negative about me and she threatened the client for disparaging her long-time friend. When the client barked back at her, she went to her car to get a crowbar and came back inside to beat her with it. Luckily a male client intervened and prevented the situation from escalating further. That was her last day.

I Didn't Want to Fire My Friend

I was highly embarrassed and in total disbelief. I didn't want to fire my friend because we had known each other for over ten years. It wasn't costing me much to have her answer the phone and the door but she was costing me my business reputation. She was definitely not the right fit for our business. Although she still wanted the job, I had to make a decision. I had to say no. I let her go.

I realized that if I brought in the right person, I would be able to bring in more clients. It couldn't be just another friend looking for a job; it had to be someone with people skills and abilities. This person will be paid from revenue she generates for the business.

And then a light bulb went on and I thought: *How can I afford NOT to bring in the right person?*

Lesson Learned: Hire the Right Person and Train Them Properly

After reflection, I knew exactly what I wanted to do:

- First, I created an *Orientation Guide* and a step-by-step *Procedure and Policy Manual* for running the front desk, including expectations and a sales quota.

- I created a job description that comprised everything I expected this person to be responsible for.

- I defined the necessary characteristics that I required of this person.

- Finally, we advertised for a receptionist.

I interviewed many before I finally found Linda. I gave her the orientation and went over everything we would expect from her, and what she could expect from us from day one.

I knew exactly what I was looking for and took approximately one month to train her to do the job correctly. It was important for me to let her see what her job looked like through my eyes, through my vision. We worked together until I was satisfied that she understood.

She dressed professionally and had a pleasant demeanor. Initially, I had her spend many hours on the phone contacting clients and rebooking the ones we had. She ran specials and became creative in bringing in new business. Over a short period of time, with her upbeat nature and love for what she did, she was able to produce an amazing amount of repeat business.

We were able to pay her a good salary from the money she brought into the school, which also helped us to take care of the many expenses we incurred. I was able to focus much more on growing the business. This is when our business began to flourish.

The Front Desk Is Your Window to the World

I have observed receptionists wasting valuable time on cell phones, playing games or reading text, talking on the phone with friends, having extensive conversations with the operators, or just sitting. This is because the owner of the business has nothing planned for them to do, and no expectations of them.

Although it might seem easy to you, take this front desk position very seriously. It is an important position for your business. I learned this the hard way.

Yes, the receptionist is being paid to answer the phone when it rings, and to sign up clients, but when there are no clients, they should have some other important tasks to do:

- They should keep the reception area inviting.

- They can make calls, asking clients if they want to re-book, reminding them of appointments or offering promotions. This kind of customer interaction can be key to keeping your business growing.

- In spare time, they can be assigned the task of following up with clients to checking their level of satisfaction.

- Ideally, a receptionist will also maintain your lists of contacts for future reference.

The front desk is your window to the world. The receptionist is likely to be the first person a client encounters. Just having the wrong person at the front desk could cripple your business.

A receptionist needs to behave professionally. To the public, they should come across as a dedicated part of the business team. They should be actively working to promote repeat business and to bring in new customers.

Observe the reception area of successful business practices, and think about how you want your reception area to run.

Set standards, write a detailed job description, and provide time for training. Follow up with meetings to assess results and answer questions.

Micromanagement

Many business owners I've met feel that they need to watch every aspect of the business. They micromanage the employees, making the employees feel uneasy. These owners feel no one can do it better than they can. Or they are afraid someone will screw up.

Instead of hovering, train your people well from the start. If you create policy and put thought and effort into training your employees, you will not need to micromanage. Take the time necessary to orient each new hire and it will save you many headaches in the end. Don't forget to schedule days to follow up on each new hire's progress so you can prevent bad habits, answer questions, and correct misunderstandings.

Train your employees to work according to *your* standards — otherwise they will work according to theirs. Give constructive criticism at the outset and support growth in an ongoing manner.

Letting employees persist in poor habits is not kind. It is detrimental to them and to your business. Encourage them to do the best they can; if they are inspired to improve, they will gain the ability to mature and grow. Help them deliver a masterpiece.

Addressing Conflict Between Employees

One of our salon clients, Tammy, contacted me because she'd had an uncomfortable experience at the salon. Her stylist had lashed out angrily at another stylist in the salon, believing that the stylist had stolen a client. It was embarrassing and awkward for everyone in the room.

When you give each employee an orientation, it should include an introduction to your policy on *business ethics*. This should lay out, among other things, proper conduct for addressing clients and other staff. It should be signed. This will eliminate any misunderstandings.

When staff members lash out against one another — or at anyone in the office, for that matter — they should be taken to your office to discuss their behavior. It should never be addressed on the floor; no matter what the issue is. After the discussion, the staff member should be given a written warning that explicitly states that this behavior will not be tolerated.

In our salon business, we also needed to detail the procedure to follow when a client chooses a different stylist. It was important enough to include in the policy handbook.

Ideally, the stylist should not take this personally; they should maintain a professional demeanor with the client and the other stylist. Instead of focusing on feelings of resentment, I encourage the stylist to consider whether he or she might need to freshen up on their practical skills or customer service. We should always be trying to improve.

MAKING CHANGES TO YOUR COMPANY

Every company can benefit from consistently researching ways to improve, then making changes at the appropriate time. Of course, you'll want to set the tone of structure and stability in your business to start, but nothing is ever carved in stone. If something isn't working, don't be afraid to make a change; after all, it's your business. You are in charge.

I'm not saying that you should constantly be changing policies; this will make it seem that you don't know what you are doing. But there are times when changes should be made.

You may want to make changes:

- To update production tools or computer software systems

- To implement new innovations or techniques

- To expand your services

- To make changes in response to the needs of clients

People often don't like change. However, change is good to stay updated on trends and ensure current systems are working to your greatest advantage. Regularly review your systems and research new ways of doing things.

If you do decide to make changes, create a schedule to allow you to the time to implement the new system correctly and to train your staff.

Making Improvements: Two Heads Are Better Than One

Create an atmosphere that welcomes suggestions for improvement and innovation.

Brainstorming about making changes can be a great team exercise, and an opportunity to help your staff members feel that they are an important part of the team. They will likely feel empowered by being invited to assist in making their own jobs more productive, and to make a difference that will help everyone.

Listen to different viewpoints; everyone has different life experience and education that will result in different perspectives. Gather them for a meeting of the minds. Consider creating a quarterly or yearly contest among your team for discovering new innovations.

Chapter Twelve

Ways to Grow Your Business

GROW YOUR LIST OF CONTACTS

Start a Blog

If you are an expert on a certain topic, others will want to listen to what you have to say. Start a blog and update it regularly.

Are you a hairstylist? Write a blog about ten ways to increase your service menu.

Are you a master gardener? Write a blog about spring gardens or how to grow tomatoes.

Are you a CPA? Write a blog about the five ways to save money on your taxes.

The Importance of Email Lists

There are automated email services that you can use as a marketing tool to keep your clients interested and to keep your business in the forefront. If you are not building an email list, you are making a huge mistake; email addresses are powerful tools for marketing.

Who should go on your list? Every person who has ever shown an interest in your service.

This list is of great value to your business. When you want to send out information on your business, you have a list of potential customers — a target audience — at your fingertips.

Many business owners who understand the importance of the list will purchase email lists of their target market. If you have an opportunity to start collecting from your current list of contacts, do so now and build, build, build.

There are email marketing service providers for businesses that are available at very low cost. Through these services, you can create different kinds of mailings, update your lists, and compile reports. *MailChimp.com* and *Constantcontact.com* are two email service sites that you may want to check out as you start your list.

Join a Professional Group

Professional business groups can be found for every field of business and are useful in many ways:

- They can be valuable sources of practical and technical information for beginning entrepreneurs and for seasoned business leaders as well.

- When you have a problem, you will be able to ask questions of people with experience in your field.

- You can build networking relationships with members that can help you with marketing your products.

- Sometimes, running a home-based business has limited social interaction. Joining a professional group can put you in touch with like-minded people. You can find many organizations relating to your particular industry by consulting with other industry professionals, industry supply stores, and trade magazines. You would be surprised at the amount of information you can obtain by simply researching online.

- It also helps to become a leader in a professional organization. Offer to assist with the organization's needs. This will allow you to know what is going on first hand, will add to your resume, and increase your value in your business field.

HONE YOUR MARKETING SKILLS

Strengthen Your Speaking Ability

As an entrepreneur, you may have an opportunity to speak at different functions. You will likely be asked to speak about your business on the phone, in person, on-stage and perhaps, in the media. Various situations and circumstances will call for your input, opinion, expertise, or dissertation. Being ready at all times is vital to your business.

Imagine you are at a social gathering and the host of the event asks you to speak about your business.

What will you say?

Rather than stumble through it making people wonder how professional you are, it's best to have it pre-rehearsed so you can speak confidently and appear like the professional you are.

There is nothing more regretful than to find yourself in the right place at the right time, and called upon to present yourself, but you can't think of much to say. Perhaps afterwards, you might realize that you left out the most important things you should have said. You would have just lost a free opportunity to advertise on someone else's platform with a captive audience.

Develop Your Thirty Second Pitch

Be ready to pitch to others who you are and what you can offer them on command. The only way to do this is to practice. Create an approach that will allow you to best describe your business in the shortest possible time frame. This is called your *thirty second pitch.*

Identify your edge — what is the advantage of working with you?

Instead of focusing on telling people that you are the best, let them know *why* you are the best. Give them your track record of accomplishments.

When someone approaches you and asks what you do, be ready to speak about yourself, without skipping a beat, for at least thirty seconds. Think it through and practice your delivery until it is seamless. Let them feel your confidence and professionalism.

Practicing what you will say will help you to build the confidence to speak with control.

Are you a nervous speaker?

When you are speaking with individuals in general, you are probably not nervous. You can speak of your children or your pet, or on other subjects you are familiar with, without stopping to read notes. You don't have to practice it because you know it.

Once you outline a speech and practice it repeatedly, like a song, it will become unconscious and automatic. You will be confident and the words will flow. Practice, practice, practice. You can also seek professional speaking courses for increased confidence.

Don't miss opportunities to speak about your business; use your voice to make a difference.

Teach a Class

Your local college or town's community center may be in need of speakers or instructors. If you look at your local town's brochure that arrives in the mail every now and then, you will see all sorts of topics being taught. When you teach a class what you know and are good at, you will get others enthused about your business too. If they can't create their own business at the moment, guess who they will call when they need that service? You!

Write a Book

Writing a book is a great way to gain attention to your company or brand. You have a book inside of you. What do you know a lot about? Can you write about a problem that you can solve? Perhaps you want to write your life story for others to learn more about you.

Set a goal to do a chapter a month or maybe five hundred words a day. Your book can be finished within two to three months. Even if it takes a year, with small advances toward the finished product, you will have a book to sell or to teach from.

Think about all of the people you could impact by teaching them something that they don't know. People will perceive you as an expert on the subject. You will also gain respect that will open doors to speaking engagements and that could catapult your growth and income.

ESTABLISHING A REPUTATION

Give It Away Until You Can Sell It

What you have to offer is only valuable to you until the day that someone else feels there is value. A major mistake that many people make is over-valuing their particular service before they have proven their value.

How can people believe your value if nobody has experienced it?

I am not necessarily telling you to give your services away for free, but it is a good idea to provide substantial discounts, if necessary, until you have created a demand for them. And sometimes you'll meet people who are worth gifting your services to. These are the people who have a large network of potential clients and are natural promoters. You'll know them by the fact that they are always telling you about good deals or good service they have received. Reward them in advance by giving them a freebie and asking them to share their experience of your good service with others.

The Best Kept Secret Is Still a Secret

People, by nature, feel that they have to see it to believe it. If you, and your services, are the best-kept secret in your business, then the secret is still a secret. How does anyone know you're as good as you say? Let them try your services.

Let them be the judge of how good it is. Give people something to go out and brag about and tell others how good your service is. If what you have is valuable, you will earn what you deserve by default.

A young girl just starting out in business was asked to volunteer by performing a presentation before a group of older people.

She refused saying, "I need to get paid for what I know. I went out and paid to learn this so no, I can't do it for free."

The one thing that I learned in business is that when you have nobody beating down the door to get to you, you go to them. You need to create a track record of success. You may not get paid in dollars, but you will get paid in other ways that bring more value than dollars. How much do you lose every day that no one knows you or your business?

How much money do you think it would be worth in free advertising to have someone validate that you are good? Perhaps you can include a testimonial or a letter of recommendation on your website and in other promotional material.

You can have your session videotaped and reproduced to sell to other audiences.

Do what you can to build your audience exposure so people will know your name or brand for future recommendation to others. You've probably received free samples many times, at department stores, supermarkets and in the mail. These are given all the time so people can get to know and trust that a product will work, and then purchase it.

Free apps for your cell phones cost thousands of dollars in hours and technology to produce, but marketers put them out there for you to try so you can see value in the service or because their use may lead to you spending money on upgrades or related services. Facebook, Twitter, Periscope and other servicers are free to you but the benefit they will get as a result of viewership outweighs the freebies. You have to think like this as an entrepreneur.

When You Need a Track Record

When we started the school, we could hardly attract any students to join our program because they did not know of the school. At the time, the competition was fierce. There were so many other schools to choose from that had more students, large campuses, exceptional track records, and financing. We enrolled two students and one dropped out, telling us that we didn't have enough students in the school.

What did we do?

Although we brought in students very slowly and we wished for more, I used this time to develop my own skills to give the very best education to the students we had. We needed to prove to ourselves that we could do it if we were willing to train the students at our highest ability, giving the very best education that we could.

This time involved a lot of learning for me. I went back to the drawing board many times while creating our strategy and approaching different challenges along the way. Over time, I gained the experience to be able to anticipate upcoming challenges and to avoid them head-on by reacting proactively. Continuous hands-on learning early in the game allowed us to build skill, strength, and character which thrust us forward. Learning from our mistakes also enabled us to help others later on.

During the early years, we gave away fourteen scholarships to attract students. We needed someone to believe in us and we needed a reputation to set us apart so we could compete with the big schools. We wanted to prove ourselves. We knew that we would not make much money at the start; but we believed in our ability and the quality of education that we would provide. We also knew that it was a chance to prove ourselves in the community. If we gave our very best to each student, we could help them to succeed and they would tell others about their experience at our school.

Remember, it doesn't matter how much money you think you should get paid; one way or another, you are still getting paid. I believe that giving is receiving and that you don't lose when you give it away. You receive the fulfillment of knowing that you have done your very best.

I loved every moment of the teaching process. I would eat, sleep, and drink the business. I looked forward to working every day. I didn't like Saturdays because it would mean that I wasn't working on Sunday or Monday. Our enrollment went from two students to over two-hundred and eighty students within three years.

When you have helped to shape someone's future by allowing them an opportunity to do their very best, you have done a great thing. Embrace giving it away and the day will come that you can sell it for what it's worth. Your joy will help you to create a reputation and eventually, a successful business. Believe in yourself.

GET PAID WHAT YOU ARE WORTH

There will come a time when your business has grown, and you realize in order to expand, you cannot continue to do it all. You have been the owner, the father and mother, the wife, the secretary, the manager, the receptionist, and the janitor.

With all of this going on, I am sure you must think at times, that you are not getting paid what you are worth.

What would you pay someone else to clean the office or answer the phone? If it is minimum wage, then this is the rate you are working for when you do it.

Certainly your time is worth more than this. At some point, you will need to hire other people so you can focus your time and attention on growing your business. You will begin to work *on* your business, not *in* your business. Business owners are leaders of thought. They think outside of the box; they are innovative and creative in finding ways to build. But if your attention stays on micro-managing the daily operation, you will never be able to harness your ideas and put them into practice.

What would it be worth to you to have someone else do those jobs, while you build your Dynasty? You deserve to get paid what you are worth. You may not be in a position to do this now, but it will come in the near future.

Should You Cut Your Prices?

Although you may at times offer promotions and discounts, these should be temporary methods to get your business some exposure. Charge for your services according to the value of the service given. Don't be afraid to set your prices for what you feel your product or service is worth. *Never* prejudge whether you think a client can afford the services you are offering. Don't blink an eye when you state your rate because you know you are giving value.

Always offer your best to everyone. You are the professional, an expert in your field, and your aim should be to please the client. Make suggestions that you know will enhance their experience. Stay firm. Don't allow yourself to be manipulated into lowering the cost of your services. Build value in yourself and your skill and they will value you.

If you are not earning the type of income that you feel you deserve, re-evaluate your skills and, if necessary, relocate to where your business can thrive.

Are You Maximizing Your Potential?

A struggling client once hired me to assess her salon and to give her pointers on how she could improve the business. I inspected the salon and discovered the operators were not maximizing the higher priced ticket services that were offered by the salon. They were not recognizing the potential to upsell.

The staff did not perform consultations at the start of the appointment. This is a missed opportunity that can minimize your earning potential. At a salon, most clients only ask for what they are accustomed to receiving without being aware that there are other services available that could enhance their beauty and image.

Become proficient at giving consultations. Offer and explain the services available. It doesn't matter if the client says no to an upgrade; just be gracious and friendly and bring them what they want. In giving the information during the consultation, you have just taken the opportunity to advertise your products, and to a person who is already comfortable with making purchases in your area of business. Don't miss this opportunity.

How do you earn more money? You continue to learn, practice and build value for your skills. Your potential earning comes from every new or enhanced skill that you add to your portfolio. Never stop learning and you will always be in demand. *If you build it*, the money will come.

Chapter Thirteen

Starting Over Again

WHEN YOU STUMBLE AND FALL

Although I had success, I also had failures. When you stumble, you have to get back up. Without failures, you cannot grow.

As I stated before, when we started our business, we struggled to make ends meet after losing our jobs. We were told that we didn't have the skills to get good paying jobs, and we fell far behind in our bills. We were at the lowest point in our lives when we applied to welfare for support; our egos were torn to shreds.

When we had an opportunity to start a business, we had to believe that it was possible even when it didn't make sense to others, because we really didn't know what we were doing. We worked hard, figured it out, and simply refused to give up. When we did create success, we made a lot of money.

We made millions. The problem was, we didn't have financial literacy to keep it, so we lost it all. I mean we had gone all the way back to barebones. We closed our business and Preston suffered a second stroke.

During this time, my daughter was getting married and I could not help her with her wedding plans because I was overwhelmed with sorrow and regret.

She sent me a copy of the invitation to her destination wedding and all I could think was: *How can we get out from under the debt we've acquired?*

I responded to her letter telling her that I was in serious debt, my utilities were turned off, the threatening calls from the bill collectors were keeping me depressed and I felt ashamed of my failures.

Once again, we hadn't have a backup plan and I was at a loss. What would I do now?

Preston's stroke was a great heartache for me. I totally shut down. I was afraid I would lose him. He wasn't even able to speak to me. I felt so alone.

Juggling our household bills and caring for him, I could not afford the mortgage payments and the upkeep of our rental properties. I tried to sell our Beauty School Building but nobody would buy it. Being forced to keep the building was a big blessing, but we didn't know this yet.

Let Go

In desperation, I wrote a letter to God: *Dear God, I don't know how we messed this up. I don't know how this will turn out, but please, give us another chance. We will do better. Please give us another chance.*

My prayer was just a few words and not well-written but I knew that God always knows my heart. He knows my pain and he knows what to do. He knows what you need before you even ask.

You don't have to use particular words to speak to God. Just ask from your heart, and then let go. He will hear you.

You don't have to go looking for Him anywhere outside of your own skin. He is there. Let go and trust in him.

When I let go, I immediately felt the change; once again, I possessed *faith on fire* and I believed with every fiber of my being that my God had an answer to my prayer, just as He had with every prayer before.

It is only when I don't trust in Him; when I try to help Him to figure it out, that I fall short. I don't have the capacity to move mountains and stop time. But He does.

Let go.

GETTING UP AGAIN

My son, Preston Jr., was away in college when he and his sister, Lakia, had a conversation about starting our business back up.

When he called me with his idea, I thought: *No, you don't understand, it will cost too much money; we don't have the ability to do it again.*

I didn't have twenty dollars saved up at the time. The place we found ourselves in with the debt and Preston's stroke had changed our lives dramatically. Our bills were behind, rental properties had gone to foreclosure, and we were living on a shoestring budget.

But our children remembered the stories I told them of victory over defeat; of how we beat the odds when we began our journey.

They asked, "What is the difference between then and now? You have already proven that being successful is possible; we already know it. It is what you taught us. It was never about having money to start, because you didn't have it in the beginning. It was about having the faith of a mustard seed and being resourceful in times of challenge. It was not about the obstacles but more about the ability to see things differently."

They wanted to do it again. Only now they wanted to partner with us and bring their knowledge to the table. They reminded me of what I always told them: *It's never too late.* They were willing to roll up their sleeves and go for it.

The thought of starting over again from scratch was scary. My fear crept in, tainting all my thoughts as I remembered all the challenges we had to overcome in the past to start a business.

I started thinking: *The technology has changed, there are more talented people in the industry, there are new standards, new business practices; In fact, everything we did to run our businesses yesterday is obsolete now.*

But one thing we had going for us was that we still owned the building that had housed the school. Then I remembered my thoughts when I first met Mrs. James, how I told her about all of the qualities I did not have to open a business. She believed in me anyway, in spite of my insecurities.

Mrs. James had moved on to Texas to be with her daughter five years after she saw the success of our business. We bought her building. But we stayed in constant contact.

Whenever too much time passed between our conversations, she would call and say, "Baby, tell me what's wrong — you have me worried about you when you don't call. I want you to call me so I will know what to ask God for!"

But I didn't want to tell her how far I had fallen down. I didn't want her to know that I had hit rock-bottom again. I didn't want her to feel that all of her work with me had gone to nothing. So I stayed away.

But after listening to Preston, Jr., I remembered her words and I picked up the phone and called her. I told her everything that had happened.

She said, "Anna, everything is in Divine Order! Keep on believing that God will work it out!"

She said she believed we could do it again and started to pray for me. I felt relieved after talking to her. I felt confident that we could do it all again. I knew that what was holding me back were my own thoughts and that I must change them myself. I started to remember: *I AM ONE with GOD!*

BETTER THAN BEFORE

I began to become inspired all over again. I started to remember our journey differently: this time, it was from another place inside me, a place of optimism and inspiration. I remembered all the steps we took, I had connections who were still available, I knew processes that had not changed, and I was a different person than I was back then.

I had years of experience that could propel our business faster than a startup. I knew exactly what to do with ideas and resources that were available, even if money wasn't. I knew where to go to get information that we needed. Over those years of being in business, I had loaded tons of unconscious mental deposits of information into my brain that I could pull from. They were like riches in the bank, just waiting for a withdrawal.

We made the decision to reinvent ourselves and to step into the arena again. The ideas began to flow. We made a plan, got focused, got started, and we became excited all over again. My

God! What a joy it is when you find that place inside that is full of confidence and courage!

Although Preston had mobility disabilities from his stroke, he, too, was optimistic that we could do it again.

I know that we have a power within that defies any logical explanation and it could move mountains. When you are pregnant with dreams that are bursting to be born, nothing will stand in the way of birth. We could see the end. It was like the beginning, we knew that we could make it happen with no reservation. And I knew exactly what to do. The adrenaline was flowing and within three years, we had done it again. We turned our lives around.

If we started over and did it again, you can too.

At some point, you will experience challenges, go through detours, roadblocks, or disappointments. But when you take that initial leap of faith, it will change your life and your world forever. It will change your path and forge the person you will become.

I realized the person I had become as a result of the journey we took was not the same person who started out so many years ago. The person I had become had built muscle of character, confidence, and faith. She knew we had everything it takes to succeed.

Our victory far out-weighed the struggle. We were blessed to know that it is possible.

You can't fail unless you give up. If you go through it once and lose it all, you already know you have what it takes to start over and do it all again. It may beat you down, but while some folks will stay down, the person you will rise-to-be will have the strength to get back up and go twelve more rounds.

Whatever you do, don't quit; pause if you must but don't stop the journey. You owe it to yourself to push past your fears.

The time is now. Let your life begin.

Open Your Mind to Possibilities

I have discovered that each of us has a power greater than we can imagine. This is something that I can't seem to describe adequately in words. It cannot be seen with the naked eye, nor reasoned with simple logic.

When you make a decision, somehow the universe will line up with your intention and cause things to happen that are not explainable.

It doesn't always come in the form of money but the results are clearly what money would have brought. It might manifest in a bill that did not have to be paid, a human angel sent to give you a ride, an unexpected statement credit, or a check in the mail you had no idea was coming, but is the answer to your prayer.

Strangers will enter your life to take part in your journey, yet they may not know why. Some will be with you for only a season, and others will be there for a lifetime. There will be situations that just don't make sense to you at the time, but you will discover later that they were a necessary part of the plan for your growth and development.

Open up and trust your inner power. When you are open to your inner power, opportunities will present themselves that you could not have imagined or dreamed of.

When you have a troubling problem that doesn't have an apparent answer, go to a quiet place and open your mind. I learned over time that answers will come to you when you engage your imagination; when you think outside your box, and step outside your comfort zone. Release the dragon!

You may think all of this talk sounds pretty bizarre. It was also strange to me, at first.

You have to look beyond your limited eyesight and seek inner vision. You must dig deeper to unveil the clarity you desire.

You will find yourself doing things you couldn't imagine before. You will come up with ideas that will startle all who know you. This ability has always been part of you. You're just now awakening to it.

There is always a way. Given the time to think it through, you can accomplish amazing achievements.

People pay hundreds of thousands of dollars to do what we did using traditional methods and little money. We were able to obtain similar or even better results than some, by employing our faith and unstoppable belief.

I've read that faith without works is dead. I know it to be true. Let your faith lead your actions.

You believe in your business, and in what is about to happen. You know that it will be a success because it just feels right inside. Before you know it, you will be attracting the right opportunities and the people who will help you. I have come to know this power operates even while we sleep. When we're quiet, we can truly hear our higher self, feeding us the truth. We wake up filled with ideas and promise.

During a moment of uncertainty, an old friend or a stranger may come along and offer to assist you, to guide you, to do something special for you, to give you something, to offer suggestions, to offer you things for free or for a fraction of what you would pay normally. You never knew these particular people would be there for you before you started your business; when you open your mind, you will find many surprises.

When you look back on your experiences from time to time, you may also discover that had you approached the opportunities negatively or with a closed mind, things may have turned out quite differently. You will also see how your life events are sequentially connected to each other.

New Doors Will Open

As one decision follows another, new doors will open as you move along.

We found that our decisions resulted in many opportunities to help other people:

- We found ourselves in a position to create jobs for many people.

- We became able to aid homeless victims by giving them free services on a regular basis.

- We began to assist unemployed persons, boosting their spirits and confidence by offering free image-development classes and services.

- We were able to give thousands of dollars in beauty school scholarships to those wanting a career.

- We were able to work with and advise people all over the world in developing and building their businesses; to consult and coach new business owners, school owners and salon owners.

Our proudest moment came when we flew our entire family and staff overseas as we opened the first cosmetology school in Togo, West Africa, a poor, under-served third-world country. We were able to send containers of beauty supplies and equipment for the students and began training the students there to be hairstylists and school owners.

The seeds we planted there continued to grow trees. To come from such humble beginnings, the enormity of our mission surprised even us.

While I was struggling in the early days, I remember others telling me to give up on the business and just get a job. I know now what I would have given up if I had taken that path.

May you open your heart and imagination to the possibilities of what lies ahead for *you*.

May you see with your vision a future filled with the freedom you seek. Stay focused; it is near.

You deserve to live on your own terms. Now, go forth and prosper!

You're worth it!

Anna

> *By any means necessary.*
> ~ Malcolm X

Everything that you have been through thus far in life has prepared you for this moment. Every trial isn't meant to persecute you; some are simply meant to prepare you for something greater in your life. Every failure is not intended for you to give up; sometimes the intentions behind the failure are to get you to give it just a little bit more.

~ Gynesis Losa Nazere

Follow your heart! Don't worry about who you were. Think about all you wish to become!

~ Kellee Patterson

We cannot solve our problems with the same thinking we used when we created them.

~ Albert Einstein

Conclusion

Congratulations! Your freedom journey has begun. I have every confidence that by adapting the information you've learned in this book, your strides will be strong and your success is inevitable. There are only a few more tips to help keep your mind on the right path:

Don't Block Your Blessings

The universe has so many blessings in store for you; you can't even imagine them all. Don't send out negative energy by focusing your time and energy on the challenge before you, on what's not working and what's out of your control. Keep your channels clear and let the positive energy flow to you and through you.

Set Your Intentions Early

Keep your eye on your destination. The road may seem far ahead of you and there may be bumps along the way, but don't let those bumps become road blocks by focusing on the wrong things. Remember, what you focus on expands.

Be Willing to Go the Distance

There are no mistakes, only results. If you don't like a result, learn from it and change it. Stay on your journey. Find ways to accept every encounter as a lesson learned. Build on this and be stronger next time, but be willing to do whatever it takes.

Marvel in the Little Miracles Along the Way

It may be an unexpected contact, a helpful phone call, a great sales day, a tip someone shared, a thoughtful gift, or a kind word someone gave at the right time. Always celebrate the unexpected miracle.

Express Gratitude Daily

Find something positive to be grateful for each and every day. When you express gratitude for even the little wins, you send positive vibes out into the universe to attract more of what you want. Don't hold grudges when things don't go as planned. At any given time, we're all doing the best we can. Send love to everyone with gratitude for each lesson you learn along your journey.

Appendix

Document Your Success

WHAT IS YOUR MOTIVATION?

Making the decision to start your own business can be difficult. Think about your own personal motivation. You must be clear about your reasons for making this move before you begin.

Here are some statements that describe the motivating factors that other people have expressed. Think about them; circle the ones that you can relate to. Below you will find space to write your own.

- I want to create my own schedule and daily routine. I want to do what I want whenever I want to do it.

- I work best alone and wish to run a business myself.

- I know that I have the ability to be my own boss. Master of my fate. I can work in an environment that allows me freedom to be myself and to express my passion.

- I don't have to put up with the sarcasm or disrespect from the people at work. I want to be treated with respect.

- I don't want to do any more of what I hate doing! No more plucking the chickens, milking the cow, working for peanuts, making the donuts, dancing for dollars, or being the organ grinder's monkey.

- I don't want to go from job to job anymore. I just want to do the one job that fits me.

- I want to do something that I love, something that brings me joy and purpose.

- I want to enhance my lifestyle.

- I will finally get paid what I am worth.

- I want to create generational wealth and a legacy for my family.

- I need the freedom to manage my own time.

- I have the experience and the ability to do my current job better, working for myself.

- I love my independence.

- I want to make a difference in the world through my passion.

- I can't stop thinking about my idea. It consumes my every thought. I have planned it for so long and now I know that I can move outside of it just being a thought and into reality.

Add more here:

_____

_____

_____

_____

_____

_____

_____

_____

_____

_____

_____

_____

_____

_____

_____

_____

_____

The people who are crazy enough to think they CAN change the world are the ones who do.

~ Steve Jobs

WAYS YOU THINK YOU WILL BENEFIT WHEN YOU START YOUR BUSINESS

- You will learn a great lesson about yourself and life.

- You will figure out cause and effect and how to start again and again from new perspectives.

- You will succeed and Life will surprise you.

- You will create wealth.

- You will become a better person, gain experience, knowledge and skills.

- You will advise others from your own experience.

- You will offer employment to others.

- You will work when, where, and if you want to.

- You will inspire & mentor others

- You will live a quality lifestyle; help and give often.

- You will leave a legacy by passing it on.

- You will change the world.

Add more here:

_____

_____

_____

_____

_____

_____

_____

_____

_____

_____

_____

_____

_____

_____

_____

_____

_____

_____

_____

_____

_____

_____

INTERVIEW YOURSELF

Now I want you to have a conversation with yourself. Think through the questions below and answer them.

1. Am I ready to start my own business?

2. Am I ready to be judge and jury for all major decisions in my business?

3. Am I willing to commit _____ hours per day to my business?

4. Am I crystal clear about what it is that I am launching?

5. Will I commit to do whatever it takes, knowing I will succeed?

6. Am I willing to give up_____ to be successful?

AND THE MOST IMPORTANT QUESTION IS . . .

When you can answer this question with total sincerity; believe at this moment that it is possible; and you know that you have the drive, determination, and motivation to stay focused and succeed; then you know you are ready to begin.

WHY DO I WANT TO BECOME A SUCCESSFUL ENTREPRENEUR?

_____

_____

_____

_____

_____

_____

_____

_____

_____

_____

_____

_____

_____

_____

_____

_____

My answer to this question — what I call my *why* — had me up at night, thinking about the possibilities. If your *why* doesn't bring you close to tears, you're not digging deeply enough.

YOUR LIFESTYLE GOALS

Imagine, for a moment, that you do not work a traditional job anymore. You have already hit your target and now you are in a position to have anything you want.

If you could wake up tomorrow morning and do whatever you want to do, what would you do? Pretend you don't have to worry about money, bills or opinions of others. What would you be doing differently and what would your lifestyle look like?

Use your imagination. Would you have a particular car, home? Vacation home? Where would it be? Would you support a particular charity? Who would you spend more time with? Where would you like to take your family? Where would you like to travel? What stores would you like to shop in?

What do you want to do with your time? Do you like skiing, crafting, golfing, dancing, spending time with loved ones, traveling? What would be your dream?

When listing your lifestyle goals, you must think as clearly as you can. You must visualize exactly what you want to happen in your life in order to set the right course to get there.

List your lifestyle goals below:

_____

_____

_____

_____

_____

_____

_____

_____

_____

_____

_____

_____

_____

_____

_____

_____

_____

_____

_____

YOUR BUSINESS ASPIRATIONS AND GOALS

Now here is the fun part. Create a list of all of the goals you would like to achieve. Think of the things that were on your list years ago. Think about what it is that you would love to do. Think about all of your talent, your passion, and your desires. What are you really good at? What is it that you could do for hours and never get bored?

Perhaps, you have many talents and ideas that you want to launch. You would like to do them all but cannot seem to make up your mind where or how to begin.

After you make the list, place a number beside each one in order of priority:

_____

_____

_____

_____

_____

_____

_____

_____

_____

_____

_____

DATE WHEN YOU WOULD LIKE THIS GOAL TO BE ACHIEVED:

Set a date. Make arrangements to start doing it now. Life *is* the journey on the way to success. When you reach that magic day, your experience of those things will be all of those days in between. Start now!

1st Date: _____

_____

2nd Date: _____

_____

TELL OTHERS ABOUT YOUR GOALS

Allowing others to know about your goal helps you to maintain focus and accountability. Be sure the people you tell are positive and desirous of your growth. Remember to surround yourself with like-minded individuals who are joyous about you reaching your pinnacle of success.

Dr. Gail Matthews, a psychologist from Dominican University in California, did a study on 267 participants, and found that people were on average 33 percent more likely to succeed in their goal if they wrote them down. Not only that, but she found that these participants were more likely to succeed if they told someone about their goal.

I will tell the following people about my goals:

First Person: _____

_____

Second Person: _____

_____

Third Person: _____

_____

SET MILESTONES

Create short-term mini-goals. Celebrate your milestone at the end of each thirty to ninety days for the first three months.

Note: You may start your planning with these worksheets, but might need to create a planning journal as your plans expand.

Milestone Day 1 _____

Milestone Day 2 _____

Milestone Day 3 _____

Space your checkpoints at thirty-day increments. Each win will increase your confidence and gets you ready for the next phase.

MID-GOAL MILESTONES

Now we will celebrate a quarterly milestone at the end of each ninety-day period.

These Are The Dates You Will Reach Each Mid-Goal Milestone:

First Quarter: _____

Second Quarter: _____

CHECKPOINT FOR MILESTONES

For each checkpoint, write down the goals you would like to accomplish during that period. Use the format listed in the next few pages as working documents to help you to achieve the goals by the deadlines you have listed above.

Duplicate the forms below as needed and complete this form for each month.

I WOULD LIKE TO ACCOMPLISH THE FOLLOWING BY THE FIRST MILESTONE:

MY DEADLINE IS: _____

_____

_____

_____

_____

_____

_____

_____

_____

_____

_____

_____

_____

_____

_____

_____

_____

_____

_____

I WOULD LIKE TO ACCOMPLISH THE FOLLOWING BY THE SECOND MILESTONE;

MY DEADLINE IS: _____

_____

_____

_____

_____

_____

_____

_____

_____

_____

_____

_____

_____

_____

_____

_____

_____

_____

_____

I WOULD LIKE TO ACCOMPLISH THE FOLLOWING BY THE THIRD MILESTONE:

MY DEADLINE IS: _____

_____

_____

_____

_____

_____

_____

_____

_____

_____

_____

_____

_____

_____

_____

_____

_____

_____

NOTES

Action Tasks   MID-LEVEL 2

**I WOULD LIKE TO ACCOMPLISH THE FOLLOWING BY
THE 2ND QUARTER**

MY DEADLINE IS: _____

_____

_____

_____

_____

_____

_____

_____

_____

_____

_____

_____

_____

_____

_____

_____

_____

_____

Action Tasks   MID-LEVEL 3

I WOULD LIKE TO ACCOMPLISH THE FOLLOWING BY THE 3RD QUARTER

MY DEADLINE IS: _____

_____

_____

_____

_____

_____

_____

_____

_____

_____

_____

_____

_____

_____

_____

_____

_____

_____

_____

_____

_____

Action Tasks   MID-LEVEL 4

I WOULD LIKE TO ACCOMPLISH THE FOLLOWING BY THE 4TH QUARTER

MY DEADLINE IS: _____

_____

_____

_____

_____

_____

_____

_____

_____

_____

_____

_____

_____

_____

_____

_____

_____

This form is to be completed for each thirty-day increment

MONTHLY REVIEW

HOW ARE YOU DOING?

_____

_____

_____

_____

_____

_____

_____

_____

_____

_____

_____

_____

_____

_____

_____

_____

_____

_____

_____

LIST THE TASKS COMPLETED

_____

_____

_____

_____

_____

_____

_____

_____

_____

_____

_____

_____

_____

_____

_____

_____

If you completed the tasks for this period, no need to read further. Continue to work on your next thirty-day set tasks.

What do you need to do to complete the tasks?

_____

_____

_____

_____

_____

_____

_____

_____

How much more time will you allow yourself to complete the tasks?

_____

_____

_____

_____

_____

_____

_____

_____

Faith, Guts, and Action

Why did you not complete the tasks?

_____

_____

_____

_____

_____

_____

_____

_____

What did you discover about you while working on these tasks?

_____

_____

_____

_____

_____

_____

_____

_____

Personal reflections:

_____

_____

_____

_____

_____

_____

_____

_____

_____

Next Steps

For inquiries regarding speaking engagements, books, CDs, or coaching, you can reach Anna Jackson at:

Mail:
Faith, Guts, and Action
29155 Northwestern HWY # 424
Southfield MI 48034-1006
Phone: 1-855-758-4378
E-mail: info@iLeadMastery.com

About the Author

Anna Jackson
Helping Others Succeed

As a business owner, published author, and consultant to business professionals throughout the region, Anna Jackson owes much of her success to perseverance and the real world experience she has gained throughout her career. Dedicated to helping others achieve their personal and business goals, Anna offers a wide range of professional consultation services.

With over thirty years of successful experience as the owner of several beauty schools and the introduction and opening of the first cosmetology school in Togo, West Africa, Anna has earned a reputation as a skilled, dedicated business professional offering others the sound business and personal advice they need for self-development and sustainability.

Anna's story began over three decades ago when her and her husband decided to capitalize on a time in their lives that was packed with self-doubt and economic stress. They decided right then and there to take a chance and work towards a brighter future for her and her family. Anna decided to open a beauty salon.

After consulting family and friends for financial backing and being turned down, Anna and her husband decided to build their business themselves. Under the guidance of Mrs. Mary James, the owner of one of the largest beauty schools in the state, Anna and Preston were able to open their own school.

The endeavor took hard work and dedication, but even through the difficult early phase, she and Preston never lost their focus on success. Within three years they went from two students over 280, and the business began to thrive. Anna and Preston worked to make their startup succeed, and their hard work and dedication paid off.

On her journey to success, Anna never gave up. She learned many valuable lessons that she now shares with others. If you are considering opening a business, expanding your current one, or just want to make changes in your life, contact Anna Jackson and let her provide the professional business and personal consulting you need to achieve your goals.

www.ingramcontent.com/pod-product-compliance
Lightning Source LLC
Chambersburg PA
CBHW070509200326
41519CB00013B/2759